Franca Falletti
(DIRECTOR OF THE GALLERY)

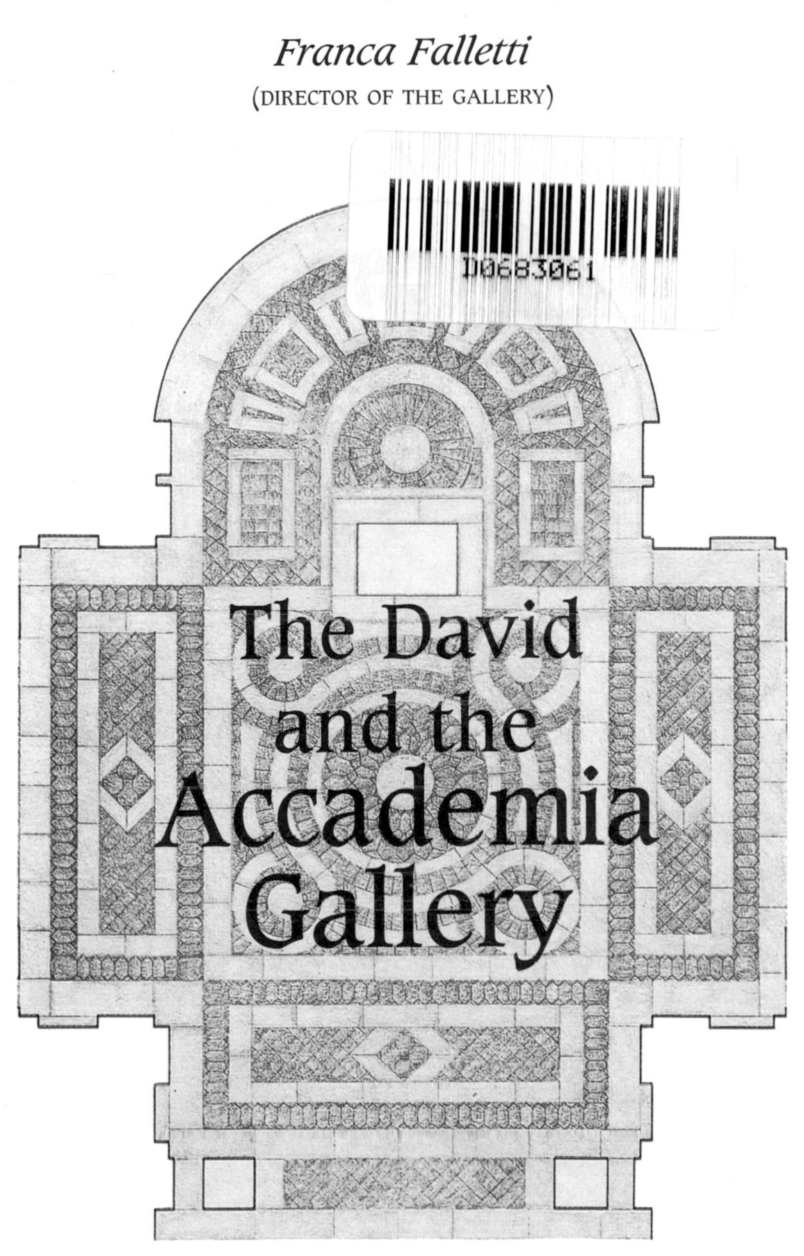

The David and the Accademia Gallery

THE TRIBUNE - FLOOR

Via dei Rustici, 5 - 50122 FLORENCE
Tel. +39 (055) 239.82.24
Fax. +39 (055) 21.63.66
E-mail: barbara@bonechi.com
bbonechi@dada.it
http://www.bonechi.com
Printed in Italy

Photos: Bonechi Edizioni "Il Turismo" S.r.l. archives: by Nicola Grifoni, Marco Rabatti and Serge Domingie, Niccolò Orsi Battaglini
U.E. Inturrisi photos n° 13 and 23
Arte Video-Genova photos n° 8,9,10,54,103
Layout, cover and drawings: Lorenzo Cerrina
Editorial supervisor: Lorena Lazzari
Translation: Julia Weiss
Photolithography: Bluprint, Florence
Printed by: BO.BA.DO.MA, Florence
ISBN 88-7204-369-7

The publishers wish to thank Ombretta Dinelli and Marco Nestucci for their kind permission to use the illustration on page 1

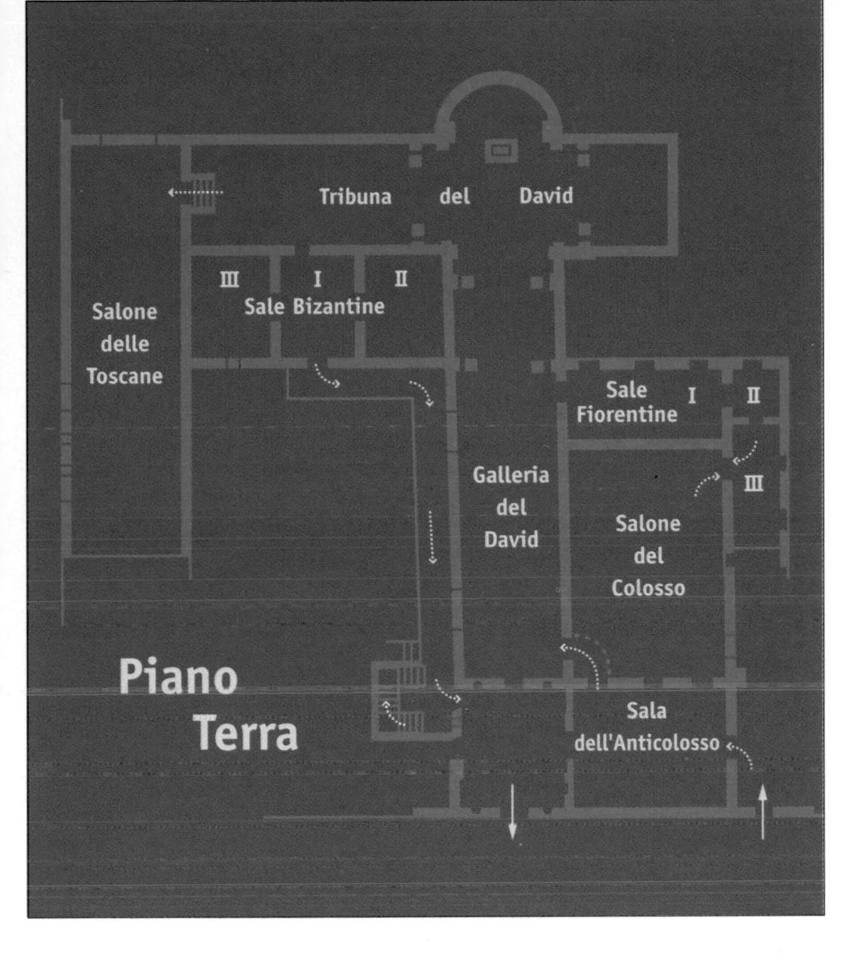

Historical Notes

The Accademia Gallery (in Italian Galleria dell'Accademia) originates from the school of fine arts which was located in the former hospital of S. Matteo where Via Ricasoli (once known as Via del Cocomero) runs into Piazza San Marco. In

1784, Pietro Leopoldo, grand duke of Tuscany founded a collection of artworks that was to provide both models and inspiration to the students. That is why, in the beginning the gallery only contained Florentine paintings from the early XIV to the late XVI centuries: the single continuous period that was believed to meet all the criteria of perfection indispensable for training young artists.
The greater part of the collection was acquired following the suppression of religious institutions under the Lorraines, then again under Napoleon and finally when Italy was united. The government, having unilaterally decided that various confraternities, convents and other religious institutions were to be closed, took possession of most of their property and added enormous wealth to its museums. The "Gallery of Modern Paintings": a group of contemporary paintings that the Grand Duke Leopoldo II acquired during the competition held in 1859 was established in 1866.
Finally, Michelangelo's David was moved to the Accademia from its original place in Piazza della Signoria in 1873. Within a few years a museum of Michelangelo's works was created, exhibiting casts of statues from other collections alongside of original sculptures such as The Prisoners and St. Matthew.
The physical transformation of the museum continued during the XX century and was accentuated between 1960 and 1980 when the David's fame began to overshadow not only the great paintings in the gallery, but Michelangelo's other works as well.
The entire first floor and the two wings on either side of the Tribune were rearranged in 1980 to provide greater interest to visitors offering a rich itinerary, while the Gallery of the Plaster Models by Bartolini and Pampaloni, famous professors at the Accademia, aimed at recreating a link with the collection's origins.
Within the next two years, the outstanding collection of historical musical instruments from the nearby Conservatorio Luigi Cherubini will be displayed in rooms connected to the Gallery. This new section will certainly enhance any visit to the Gallery.
Today the Accademia Gallery is the fourth most popular museum in Italy, and its collection of Michelangelo's sculptures is, without doubt, unequalled by any museum in the world.

1

The Gallery and the Tribune

This monumental room was designed by the architect Emilio De Fabris after Michelangelo's David was moved from Piazza Signoria to the Accademia in 1873. It was officially opened in

1882 following many discussions and conflicts, and it soon became a real "Museum of Michelangelo": alongside of the originals there were also plaster casts of works in other collections so that the documentation on the artist could be considered quite complete. Even today, with the four Prisoners, Saint Matthew and the David, the Gallery and the Tribune comprise a significant collection that is capable of arousing incomparable feelings in those who are fortunate to see it.
For a fuller appreciation of Michelangelo's Florentine works, visit the Museo di Casa Buonarroti and the Medici Chapels.

Michelangelo Buonarroti - (Caprese 1475-Rome 1564)
1 - *Prisoner* or The Young Slave. Inv. Sculptures n° 1080.
2 - *Prisoner* or The Awakening Slave. Inv. Sculptures n° 1078.
3 - *Prisoner* or The Bearded Slave. Inv. Sculptures n° 1081.
4 - *Prisoner* or Atlas. Inv. Sculptures n° 1079.
The four statues are situated along the right and left walls of the Gallery. St. Matthew stands on the right, between the The Young Slave and The Bearded Slave. The "Prisoners" group was commissioned in 1505 as part of the plans for the grandiose tomb for Pope Julius II. Originally designed as a majestic complex to be situated at the intersection of the nave and transept in St. Peter's in the Vatican, over the years it was modified and changed so many times that it caused Michelangelo considerable anguish. Finally, the last version, much changed, diminished and distorted was placed in S. Pietro in Vincoli where it stands today, and where there was no room for any of the Prisoners that are now in the Accademia, or for the two which are in the Louvre.
Michelangelo carved the Prisoners not long before he definitively moved to Rome in 1534. After his departure the four statues were left in his Florence home and in 1564 his nephew Leonardo gave them to the grand duke Cosimo I who, in turn, had them moved to the Grotta del Buontalenti in the Boboli Gardens. They stayed in the artificial "grotto until 1909 when they were replaced by copies and moved to shelter inside the Gallery.
Of all Michelangelo's sculptures the Prisoners, perhaps, best convey the meaning of "unfinished" and the relationship between the artist and his work. There is no doubt that, although the troubles and conflicts surrounding the monument could have influenced the fact that he never completed

2

the Prisoners, Michelangelo had always intended to stop work when he did, and leave the statues at the point of maximum expressive power, without worrying about the final finishing. The reason being that, the more defined and detailed a concept is, the more restricted its potential significance and

3

meaning, whereas, when it is less defined the human spirit can attribute a broader range of meanings to it. The Prisoners, created to symbolize man struggling to free himself from the bonds of sin - from which only Catholic Doctrine could provide release - (this was supposed to be their meaning in the mon-

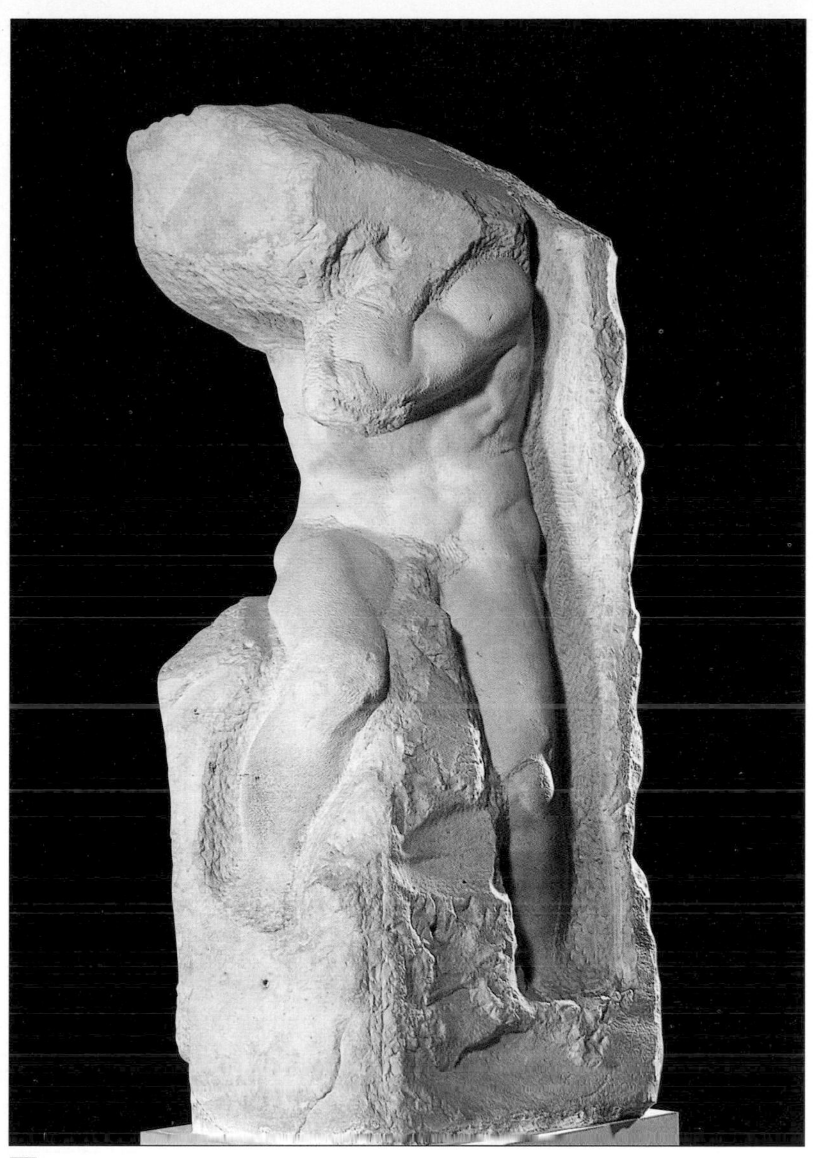

4

umental tomb of Julius II), that were not finished or placed in their original context, have become the symbol of man trying to free himself from the chains of the human condition. It is for this reason that the Prisoners are among the few artworks in the world that have always been admired and understood

5

in every era and in spite of changing trends and tastes. Even today, they strike the soul of modern man because they embrace deep and unchanging problems. Therefore, the artist's task is not necessarily that of finishing a project, but of carving, and removing material (in this case, marble) until the Idea can emerge and show itself in all its power.

5 - *St. Mattew*. Inv. Sculptures n° 1077.
Michelangelo received the commission for this statue in 1503, it was to be the first of a series of twelve that were to go decorate the pillars in the Florence Cathedral. Actually, the project was abandoned sometime after the St. Matthew was completed between 1505 and 1506 and the statue was left in the courtyard of the Opera del Duomo until 1831 when it was moved to the Accademia and then put into the Gallery.
Like the Prisoners, St. Matthew is unfinished, but the feeling of an intense and dramatic internal struggle emerges fully. The contrast between the materia! and the Ideal, between the limit and the infinite, between the heavy bonds of human nature and the yearning for divine perfection are all nearly tangible in the twisted and gnarled figure of the Apostle. This statue can be compared to Giambologna's Rape of the Sabines in the Colossus room. Giambologna, a sculptor in the pure Mannerist style, used the same types of shapes (spiraling and counterbalanced), but the intent was to show off his artistic skill and virtuosity. The twisted and entangled limbs were created to astound the viewer with technical daring and the esthetic power of the composition. The extended neck muscles of St. Matthew, the arm, forcibly moved backward, almost pulling away from the bent leg, are an incarnation of the human soul's inner torment.

6 - *Palestrina Pietà*. Inv. Sculptures n° 1319.
This statue, which the Italian government purchased in 1939 comes from the Barberini Chapel at Palestrina. It is not mentioned in any of the documentary sources about the artist and this has raised some doubts about its authenticity. However, other considerations have led more recent critics to contest it and deny that is Michelangelo's. The marble itself is antique and was being "recycled". On the left there is a fragment of an architectural decoration that was probably part of the structure it was taken from, its flat shape forced the artist to squeeze the group into two parallel planes, preventing the twisting movement that is so typical of Buonarotti's other works. This Pietà faces front, and is therefore, totally static and a complete antithesis to Michelangelo's poetry. In addition, certain "errors" of proportion in the limbs would suggest that it was carved by a member of Michelangelo's circle of followers rather then by the master himself (note the obvious inconsistency between the

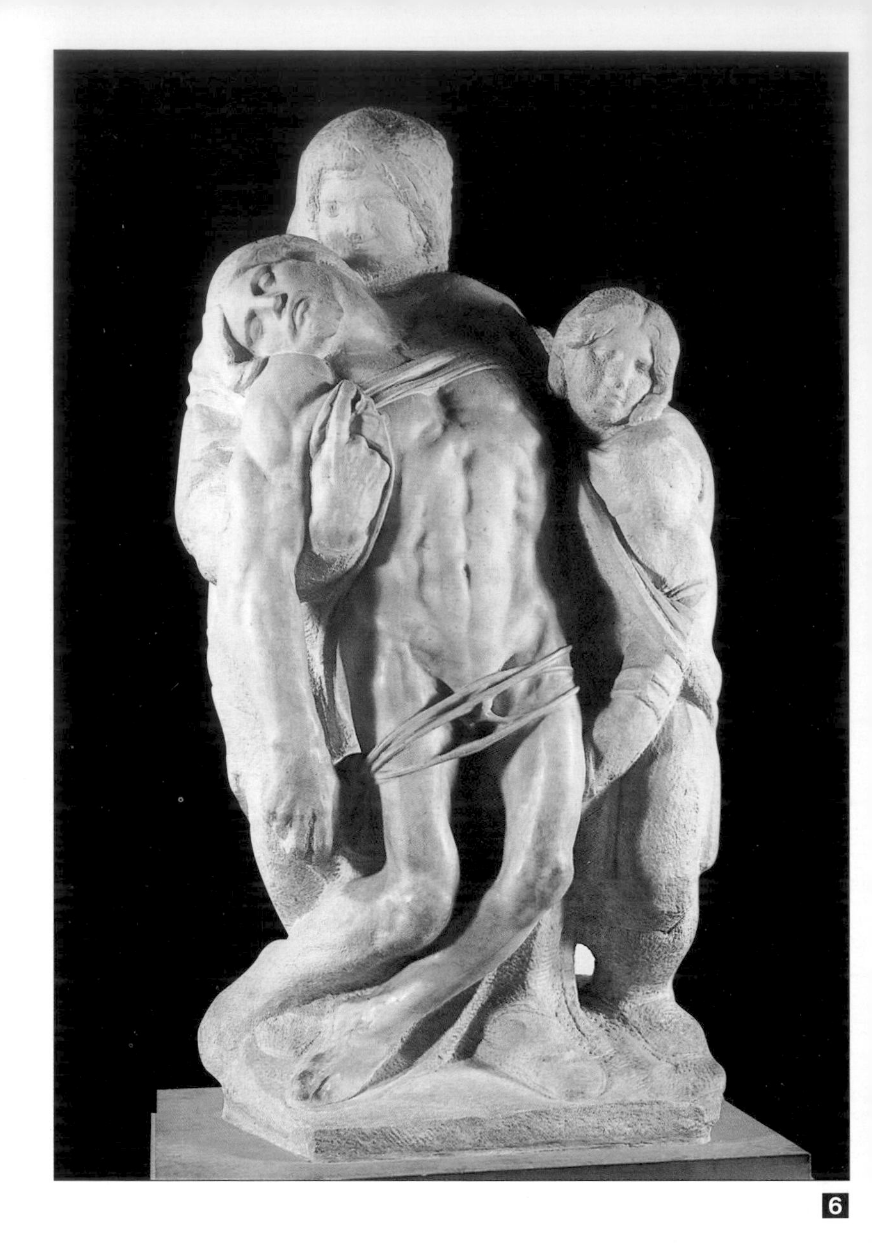

6

thin, short legs of the Christ figure and his powerful torso). The Palestrina Pietà does, however, provide strong evidence of the attention Michelangelo's artistic contemporaries dedicated to his work and at the same time reveals how difficult it was to copy, since it was not based so much on physical models, but on

7

profound spiritual experiences which belonged only to the artist himself.

7 - *David*. Inv. Sculptures n° 1076.
The David was ordered by the Opera del Duomo di Firenze in

1501 after Agostino di Duccio and Antonio Rossellino in 1463-64 and 1476, respectively had both tried and given up trying to carve that block of marble. They had come up against enormous technical difficulties since its shape was not at all in harmony with the subject and furthermore it had several flaws. By 1504 he had completed the statue except for the finishing. A committee was appointed to decide where to put it: the greatest doubts centered on whether to leave such a delicate and porous material exposed to the elements. In fact, the first serious damage to the David was done in 1527 when, shortly after being placed outside Palazzo Vecchio (Piazza Signoria), it was pelted with stones during a riot. The left arm and hand were broken into several pieces. The grand duke, Cosimo I, ordered repairs done immediately, but the signs of the damage can stili be seen today.

Towards the middle of the nineteenth century arguments about the safety and preservation of the David became more intense, especially in view of the approaching four-hundredth anniversary of Michelangelo's birth (1875) when a great commemorative exhibition was planned. Another committee was formed, and this one found such damage that it recommended moving the statue indoors. And so, in 1873 the David was moved to the Accademia di Belle Arti where the architect Emilio De Fabris designed and built the covered Tribune where the statue still stands today. The David's fame has grown disproportionately in recent years to the extent that it has reached fanatic extremes. This culminated on 12 September 1991 when a highly disturbed individual struck the second toe of the left foot with a hammer. The episode aroused public outrage around the world and made people reflect on the dangers inherent in over idealization whether it be direct towards people or works of art.
The fact remains that the David is one of the emblems of

Western art, full of new symbolism, ethical and social meaning and a groundwork for future developments in the history of art. The symbolic innovations are evident when we compare Michelangelo's David with the one by Donatello in the Bargello. Here the Biblical hero is shown as a mature youth rather than as an adolescent as the Bible would have. This corresponds to the esthetic decision of using classical size models, but it also means the dominance of an ideal beauty as opposed to the historical reality. And in the final analysis, this masks the abandonment of humanistic classicism (the return to the principles, ideals and inner tensions of the classic world) and the opening towards Renaissance humanism (the relationships, functions and modes of the classic world).

The David also opened new perspectives from the technical standpoint. The new way of handling the marble, to create the feeling of bare skin, the slingshot (note the contrast between the rough leather strap and the youth's smooth back), and finally the realistic tree trunk behind the right leg: are all a prelude to Mannerist virtuosity and the superficial effects of Baroque sculpture.

Nor can we ignore the greatest of Michelangelo's symbolic innovations: his David is not resting his foot on the slain Goliath's head. And we cannot even say that he is portrayed right before he struck because he is not holding the stone in his hand. The statue is in a static pose; and finally, ancient sources describe him as crowned with laurel like the triumphant classical hero. In Michelangelo's statue we can see the obvious intent to merge the classic model of the laurel-crowned athlete with the Biblical defender of the faith. Once again there is the desire to bring classical culture together with religion: the constant fixed reference throughout Michelangelo's life. In this specific case the need was almost absolute since the subject which had been chosen by the

Opera del Duomo for the cathedral was then placed in front of Palazzo Vecchio giving it a secular significance. It practically became the symbol of the Fiorentine people's civic liberty and a warning to those who would attempt to threaten that supreme value.

The Florentine Rooms

The series of XV century Florentine paintings in these rooms provide a concise but full summary of the work done in the local ateliers during the era of Masaccio, Piero della Francesca and Botticelli. Rather then a grouping of masterpieces, it is an outline of a historical and cultural context with the various trends that characterized the birth and development of the early Renaissance in Florence.

There are excellent opportunities to learn more about fifteenth century Florentine painting in the Uffizi Gallery, Museo di San Marco (Beato Angelico), Church of Santa Maria del Carmine

8

(Masaccio), Palazzo Medici Riccardi (Benozzo Gozzoli), Cenacle of Santa Apollonia (Andrea del Castagno), and the Church of Santa Maria Novella and the cloisters (Paolo Uccello).

8 - **Mariotto di Cristofano** (S. Giovanni Valdarno 1393-Florence 1457)
Scenes from the Life of Christ and the Virgin. Inv. 1890 n° 8508.
This panel, which comes from the church of S. Andrea at Doccia near Florence was recently attributed to Mariotto di Cristofano, an artist whose style was close to Beato Angelico, as can be seen in the modes and ideas of this painting. The entire format, with the rectangles containing the individual scenes, recalls the decorations on the "Silver" chest in SS Annunziata that Beato Angelico did sometime after 1450.

9 - **Andrea di Giusto Manzini** (Florence, first half of XV cent.)
Madonna of the Girdle with Saints. Inv. 1890 n° 3236.
Dated 1437 and signed "Andrea de Florentia", this painting comes from the church of Sta Margherita at Cortona (Arezzo). It depicts the Virgin, flanked by St. Catherine of Alexandria and

9

St. Francis, giving her girdle to St. Thomas.
The artist, Andrea di Giusto Manzini, who worked with Paolo Uccello on the frescoes in the Prato cathedral, was active in Florence in the first half of the fifteenth century; he was greatly influenced by Beato Angelico, but was also sensitive to the styles of Masaccio and Masolino.

10 - Maestro dell'Epifania di Fiesole (Florence, second half of the XV cent.)
Coronation of the Virgin. Inv. 1890 n° 490.
The painting, of unknown provenance, was done by an artist whose identity is still uncertain (perhaps Filippo di Giuliano). The name which has been given to him (Maestro dell'Epifania di

10

Fiesole) comes from an Adoration of the Magi in the church of S. Francesco at Fiesole which he supposedly painted. The cultural context in which this refined artist developed and worked is readily defined: between Cosimo Rosselli, to whom the painting had long been attributed, and Jacopo del Sellaio whose influence can be seen in the angels above the two main figures; the minute and smooth face of the Virgin would create a link with the style of Alessio Baldovinetti.
The strained, austere face of the Christ, on the other hand, reveals northern European (specifically German) influences which contemporary prints were beginning to spread through Italy during the artist's era.

11 - **Domenico di Michelino** (Florence 1417-1491)
The Three Archangels and Tobias. Inv. 1890 n° 8624.
This painting comes from the church of Sta Felicita where there was an active cult of the Archangel Raphael, following his mirac-

11

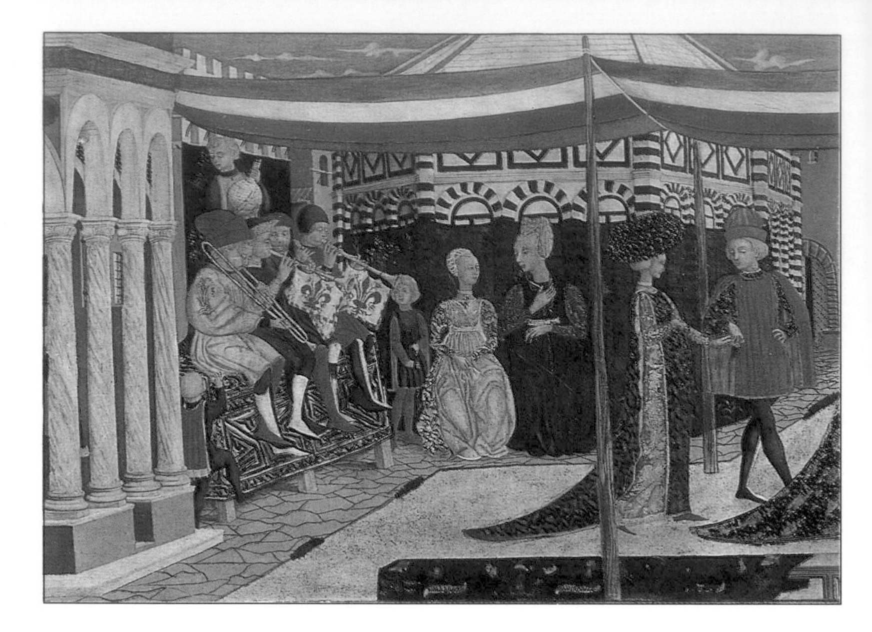

ulous apparition in 1424. The painting was probably ordered by a certain Michele di Corso, who was patron of the altar dedicated to the saint and archangel. The date was around 1465 as evi-

denced by the striking similarities with the fresco depicting Dante and the Divine Comedy in the cathedral, the most famous work by this relatively mediocre artist who, along with Mariotto di Cristofano, typified mid-fifteenth century Florentine painting styles.

12 - **Lo Scheggia** (Giovanni di Ser Giovanni, San Giovanni Valdarno 1406-Florence 1486)
Wedding Scene (Adimari) Inv. 1890 n° 8457.
The painting was acquired on the private market in 1826 and was originally believed to trave been the front of a chest made for the wedding of Lisa Ricasoli and Boccaccio Adimari (22 June 1420). This hypothesis, however, did not last very long since the style of the work dates it around the middle of the century. Actually, it is not even the front-piece of a chest, but rather a " spalliera " that is, an item used in the more luxurious palaces to decorate the upper part of a wall. This panel is one of the liveliest and most delightful scenes of fifteenth century Florentine life: well-detailed costumes (note the round hat made of peacock feathers) and minute attention to the city scene (the baptistery on the left, in the background, and then the city walls, and the landscape dotted with villas far behind). The artist who did this painting was only identified recently, he was Giovanni di Ser Giovanni, nicknamed Lo Scheggia, and was, in fact, Masaccio's brother.

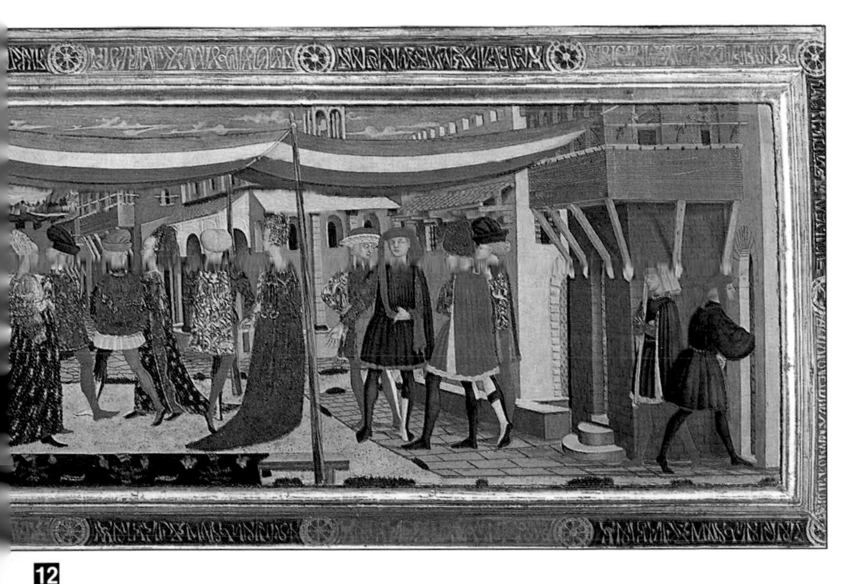

12

13 - **Maestro della Natività di Castello** (Florence, mid-XV cent.)
Nativity. Inv. Storage n° 171.
This painting was found in 1903 in one of the rooms at the Medici Villa at Castello, but this was not its original setting since the coats of arms (no longer visible) of the Medici and Tornabuoni families were originally at the base. Therefore, it must have been ordered by Piero de'Medici known as Piero the Gouty and Lucrezia Tornabuoni, who did not own the villa. The Castello estate was purchased by their cousins, Lorenzo and Giovanni di Pierfrancesco in 1477.

13

The anonymous master who painted this Nativity scene - that also gives him a name of sorts - was a Florentine artist who worked around the mid XV century (the piece can be dated between 1455 and 1460) loyal to the styles of Filippo Lippi, Gozzoli and Pesellino.

14 - **Gherardo di Giovanni** (Florence 1445-1497)
Virgin Enthroned with Child and Saints. Inv. 1890 n° 9149.
This is one of the few known paintings by Gherardo di Giovanni who otherwise illuminated manuscripts. He and his brother, Monte, had a workshop below the church of the Badia Fiorentina. The skilled illuminator's hand shows in the attention to the decorative details, such as cloak of St. Louis or the trimming on St. John's robes, with golden letters that appear to be the "Incipit" of an illuminated manuscript. There is also a bit of awkwardness in the larger spaces and there is a lack of any convincing relationship between the figures. The elements that comprised Gherardo's background can be readily defined: Ghirlandaio's and Botticelli's influence show up in the Virgin and the saints, while the plasticity of the Child's limbs was clearly inspired by Verrocchio.

14

15 - **Botticelli?** (Alessandro Filipepi, Florence 1445-1510)
Madonna of the Sea. Inv. 1890 n° 8456.
This painting was brought to the Accademica from the convent of Sta Felicita when the state repossessed it in 1810. Its name comes from the seascape behind the figure of the Virgin: it has long been an object of attention, because of its delicacy and the charming melancholy, slightly bewildered look of the young maternal figure. Critics, however, trave not definitively attributed the painting to Botticelli; originally it was defined as his, or from his school, and then later the so-called "Friend of Sandro", probably Filippo Lippi, but not all critics agree on this. There are certain similarities to

15

Lippi's work. The use of a soft. not yet taut outline and the marine background that evokes a feeling of Leonardo da Vinci would lead to a dating between 1475 and 1480.

16 - **Filippino Lippi** (Prato 1457-Florence 1504)
Maestro della Natività Johnson (Florence, second half of the XV cent)
Annunciation. Inv. 1890 n° 4632.
This painting, from the church of S. Firenze is a copy of the Annunciation that Filippo Lippi had done for the Murate monastery and which is now in Munich. It is quite evident that two different artists worked on it: Filippino Lippi most probably did the entire figure of the Virgin and the face of the Angel, while the rest was completed by the artist known as "Maestro della Natività Johnson", perhaps Domenico di Zanobi, a pupil and helper of Filippo Lippi. We know that from 1467 on he had an atelier in Via delle Terme where he worked with Domenico di Michelino. The style of the painting makes it datable around 1475.

16

17 - Sebastiano Mainardi? (San Gimignano 1466-Florence 1513)
Lamentation. Inv. 1890 n° 8623.

This painting, which comes from the convent of San Girolamo sulla Costa in Florence has been attributed to one of the many Florentine painters who worked in Domenico Ghirlandaio's atelier, and have often been confused with him such as Bartolomeo di Giovanni, Gherardo di Giovanni and the Maestro dell'Epifania di Fiesole. This all confirms Ghirlandaio's enormous influence on Florentine artistic life in the last quarter of the XV century when he was the head of a large and perfectly organized business that included painters of great skill in panel and fresco painting (Mainardi himself was distinguished in both). Mainardi, who came from near Siena was particularly gifted in creating colors. His hand is recognizable in the transparent brush strokes of his

17

purple and leaden tones. Where the colors are worn through, it is possible to see that the arms were initially painted in a different position.

18 - **Gherardo di Giovanni** (Florence 1445-1497)
The Virgin Adoring the Child. Inv. 1890 n° 8634.
This painting comes from the church of Santissima Annunziata, along with many others that were brought to the Gallery when religious orders were suppressed. After having been attributed to Cosimo Rosselli's workshop this little panel was definitely assigned to Gherardo di Giovanni del Fora, illuminator and painter, and brother of Monte who made some of the stupendous missals that are in the Museo del Bargello. The two brothers began their careers in a workshop below the Badia Fiorentina,

18

19

along with their third brother, Bartolomeo, from whom they split after some conflicts about their work. They lived their whole lives in a house on the corner between Piazza San Marco and Via Larga (today Via Cavour) where, even today, there is a tabernacle with the Virgin painted by Gherardo.

19 - **Paolo Uccello** (Paolo di Dono, Florence 1397-1475)
Scenes of Hermit Life. Inv. 1890 n° 5381.
The canvas reached the Accademia in 1810 from the Vallombrosian monastery of S. Giorgio alla Costa. However, it is very likely that originally it was in a Franciscan monastery, perhaps that of S. Gerolamo and S. Francesco, on the Costa and adja-

19 (details).

cent to the monastery of S. Giorgio. Starting from the top the painting shows St. Francis receiving the stigmata, St. Jerome adoring the Crucifix, the Virgin appearing before St. Bernard and St. Benedict who is preaching the rule to his followers. The subject is not entirely clear, but it does refer to the ideal road to perfection to attain direct participation in the Sacrifice of Christ (St. Francis' stigmata).
The painting has long been attributed to the school of Paolo Uccello, or to artists close to him, but recent criticism opts directly for the master, in a later part of his life, around the 'seventies, due to an affinity with other works from that period, and in particular "A Hunt in a Forest" (Oxford).

20 - **Alessio Baldovinetti** (Florence 1425-1499)
The Holy Trinity with St. Benedict and St. Giovanni Gualberto.
Inv. 1890 n° 8637.

Earlier cleansing with strong corrosives devastated this painting's colors and in some places permanently ruined the surface. However, the large altarpiece is still an important part of late fifteenth century visual arts. It was on the high altar of the church of Sta Trinita, and had been commissioned by Borgianni dei Gianfigliazzi, patron of the chapel, on 11 April 1470. The painting was moved from its original position in 1671 and was replaced by the cross of St. Giovanni Gualberto from S. Miniato al Monte. First it was on a wall of the apse, then in the Sacristy and in 1810 was brought to the Accademia under the Napoleonic supression of religious orders. In addition to its historical importance, Baldovinetti's panel is remarkable for its complex spatial structure which was created without any reference to landscapes, and thus exclusively through the positions of the figures (note the angels, some facing front and others with their backs turned)

20

and their arrangement on successive planes (such as Christ Crucified and The Father).

21 - **Pietro Perugino** (Pietro Vannucci, Citta della Pieve c. 1448-Fontignano 1523)
Visitation. Inv. 1890 n° 8654.
This small painting came to the Accademia when the convent of the Dominican sisters of the Crocetta in Florence was closed; however, this was not its original site since the convent was only established in 1511. The small scene of the Stigmata of St. Francis in the background has led experts to believe that it was originally in a Franciscan monastery. Previously attributed to Jacopo del Sellaio and Ghirlandaio, today's critics believe it was done by the young Perugino around 1472, the year he arrived in Florence.
The painting, that was evidently part of a predella, recalls the style of Domenico Ghirlandio and Andrea del Verrocchio whom Vasari mentioned as Perugino's teacher. However, there is no lack

21

22

of elements typical of the Umbrian master especially in the luminous and meticulously drawn landscape, as well as the expanded, but physically definable space.

22 - **Domenico Ghirlandaio?** (Domenico Bigordi, Florence 1449-1494)
St. Stephen with Saints Jacopo and Peter. Inv. 1890 n° 1621.
This painting had previously been attributed to Sebastiano Mainardi, a painter of Ghirlandaio's circle, but more recent critics, recognizing a much better quality, have come to consider it a work of the master. It was commissioned by Stefano di Jacopo Boni in 1493 for the family chapel in the church of S. Maria Maddalena de' Pazzi in Florence, a short time later, perhaps in 1513, but not later than 1524 it was moved to the chapel of St. Jerome, and, St. Stephen was painted over as St. Jerome, it is said by Fra Bartolomeo. Unfortunately, this addition, that could

23

have been quite valuable was removed during a nineteenth century restoration.

23 - Lorenzo di Credi (Florence c. 1456/5-1537)
Nativity. Inv. 1890 n° 8661.
Most probably the painting comes from the church of SS Annunziata where, on the altar in the Chapel of the Blessed Giovacchino Piccolomini, there is another painting of the same subject by Lorenzo di Credi. It is a typical, late fifteenth "mixture" of a Nativity and Adoration of the Child, and in this particular version the other figures in addition to the Virgin and two angels are St. Joseph, who is sometimes replaced by St. Giovannino.
A stylistic analysis of the background landscape, with some Flemish elements and the refined, intellecutalized architecture would date the painting between 1480 and 1490.

24 - **Cosimo Rosselli** (Florence 1439-1507)
St. Barbara with St. John the Baptist and St. Matthew. Inv. 1890 n° 8635.

The painting was brought from the chapel of Saints Barbara and Quirico in the SS Annunziata; the chapel belonged to the Teutonic nation which included the German and the Flemish peoples: the painting was there until 1740 when the chapel was radically remodelled and Rosselli's work was replaced by one by Giuseppe Grisoni. It can be dated around 1470 because of specific stylistic and iconographic characteristics: the artist was lively and very aware of this contemporary Florentine surroundings. There is an obvious link to the altarpiece by Piero and Antonio del Pollaiolo for the chapel of the "Portugese Cardinal" in S. Miniato al Monte, completed in 1468. These resemblances can be seen in the overall structure and the colored marble floor, while the warrior trodden by the Saint rccalls the figure Ghirlandaio painted for the church of S. Andrea a Cercina in 1470 The incisive lines also evoke the style of Andrea del Castagno,

24

especially in the two lateral saints: while the decorations on St. Barbara's robes reflect the rich and sumptuous tastes of the period.

25 - **Bartolomeo di Giovanni** (Florence, data from 1488 to 1501)
St. Jerome, The Stigmata of St. Francis, Deposition. Inv. 1890 n° 8627, 8628, 8629.
These three small paintings are actually compartments of a predella, a genre in which this artist, who was trained in Ghirlandaio's atelier, was specialized. Actually, his style was very similar to the

25

master's as well. His historical identity with a certain Giovanni di Bartolomeo di Domenico whose workshop was located on the Canto de' Pazzi, and was buried in the nearby church of Santa Maria in Campo in 1501 was only recently confirmed. For a long time he had been confused with another Bartolomeo di Giovanni, brother of Gherardo di Giovanni two of whose works are also displayed in this room (The Virgin Adoring the Child and the Virgin Enthroned with the Child and Saints).

26

26 - **Botticelli** (Alessandro Filipepi, Florence 1445-1510)
Madonna and Child, St. Giovannino and Two Angels. Inv. 1890 n° 3166.
This painting comes from the old Florentine hospital of Sta Maria Nuova and is almost unanimously believed to be by Botticelli. Chronologically, it belongs to a very early period in his career. somewhere around 1468. as revealed by the formal similarities with analagous works by Filippi Lippi, who was Botticelli's teacher from 1465 to 1467. However, there are also evident links to the style of Andrea del Verrocchio, especially in the face of St. Giovannino standing behind and to the right of the Virgin. The lines are decisive and the surfaces taut and compact, almost metallic and quite different from the softer forms of Botticelli's mature works.

27 - **Botticelli's Atelier** (Florence, late XV cent.)
Virgin Enthroned with Child and Saints. Inv. 1890 n° 4344.
The Madonna and Child, surrounded by Saints Dominic, Cosma

27

and Damian (on the left) and John the Baptist, Lawrence and Francis (on the right) was originally done on wood panels, like most fifteenth century paintings, but was transferred to canvas during a restoration. It comes from the oratory annexed to the Trebbio estate in the Mugello district, which belonged to the Medici family until 1644.
The original Medici ownership is also confirmed by the images of Saints Cosma and Damian, the family's patron saints. The purchaser was probably Lorenzo di Pierfrancesco, an educated and refined member of the family's younger branch, since it is listed in an inventory of 1498. This also explains the figures of St. Lawrence and St. Francis. The painting does deviate somewhat from Botticelli's style: saints Lawrence and Dominic are better than the Madonna and Cosma and Damian and these considerations caused a shift in attribution to the atelier and away from the master's own hands. Chronologically it still belongs in the fourteen eighties.

28 - **Raffaellino del Garbo** (Raffaellino de'Carli, Florence 1466-1525)
Resurrection. Inv. 1890 n° 8363.
This panel, in its elaborate frame is a highly documented and frequently mentioned work by Raffaellino de' Carli, also known as Del Garbo, from the street where his workshop was located. Vasari, in his *Lives*, mentions that the large painting adorned the chapel that the Florentine noble family Capponi had built under the church of S. Bartolomeo at Monteoliveto; the chapel was known as "Il Paradiso" because of its lovely surroundings. Vasari also tells us that the young sleeping warrior with his hand under his cheek is actually a portrait of Niccolò Capponi.
The panel was removed from its original setting in 1810 in accordance with Napoleon Bonaparte's orders to close the convents and monasteries and by 1813 it was already on exhibit in the Accademia.
Since its earliest days it had been considered one of Raffaellino's most intense and greatest works, but its chronology is still open to debate.
Some critics tend to place it among his earlier works (before 1500) as Vasari himself suggested, while others prefer a date somewhere around 1505/1506. In fact, along with the influence of Filippino Lippi who had been his teacher and never completely forgotten, we can see the softness typical of Perugino whom Del Garbo studied only in the early years of the new century. And

28

mainly, it is impossible to believe that some of the figures, such as the kneeling warrior on the left. were conceived without the influcncc of Leonardo da Vinci and his cartoons for the Battle of Anghiari (1504).

29

Colossus

This large room is named after the plaster copy of one of the Dioscuri of Monte Cavallo near Rome which had been placed here in the XIX century. Today, it contains paintings by early sixteenth century Florentine Painters such as Fra Bartolomeo, Andrea del Sarto, and Perugino. It is a significant prelude to Michelangelo's majestic works in the Gallery and the Tribune.
For a better understanding of early sixteenth century painting in Florence: Uffizi Gallery, Palatine Gallery, Cloister of the Scalzo (Andrea del Sarto) and the Cenacle of San Salvi.
For a fine overview of sixteenth century sculpture in Florence: Museo Nazionale del Bargello and Piazza Signoria.

29 - **Giambologna** (Jean de Boulogne, Douai 1529-Florence 1608)
Rape of the Sabines. Inv. Sculptures n° 1071.
Giambologna was a Flemish sculptor who came to Florence some time around 1554, the " Rape of the Sabines " dates from 1582. The statue here is the full-size plaster model of the marble original which stands in the Loggia dei Lanzi (Piazza Signoria). Originally the group was meant to be a display of the artist's skill with marble (it was named about a hundred years later), since he had already acquired a reputation for making bronze statues. The complex group develops upwards in a spiral so that it can be viewed from any side creating equal effects according to the then new principles of Mannerist figurative language.

30 - **Mariotto Albertinelli** (Florence 1474-1515)
Annunciation. Inv. 1890 n° 8643.
Ridolfo del Ghirlandaio (Florence 1483-1561)
Miracle of St. Zanobi and Translation of the Saint's Body. Inv. 1890 n° 1504, 1589.
This grandiose altarpiece by Albertinelli comes from the Confraternity of San Zanobi that was located in the presbytery of the Florentine cathedral. It is dated 1510 and was paid for in installments between 1506 and 1511. The painting is a "summa" of the various trends that intertwined and developed during those crucial years of the early sixteenth century in Florence. The artist created a blend of shadings taken from Leonardo, sweet classicism in the manner of Raphael and the monumentality of Fra Bartolomeo with whom he worked during that period. Ridolfo del

Ghirlandaio completed the altarpiece after Albertinelli's death with the two scenes depicting the Miracle of St. Zanobi and the Translation of the Saint's Body that have finally been put back together with the central part. Ridolfo's panels were praised by his contemporaries who criticized the "cloudy" nature of Albertinelli's work. In fact, Albertinelli's paintings did not benefit from contact with the more modern pictorial trends, while Ridolfo's clean, solid fifteenth century classicism, barely touched by a more solid and monumental note, expressed its full potential in these works.

30

31 - **Giovanni Antonio Sogliani** (Florence 1492-1544)
Dispute About the Immaculate Conception. Inv. 1890 n° 3203.
Giovanni Serristori ordered the altarpiece for the church of S. Francesco all'Osservanza, on the hill of S. Miniato near Florence. The painting never reached its destination because the customer died before it was completed and his son-in law Alammano di Jacopo Salviati gave it to the nuns in the Convent of S. Lucia in Via S. Gallo.
The complex iconography portrays the Doctors of the Church in front of the body of Adam discussing the Immaculate Conception of the Virgin. The issue was very current in those days, partly

31

because of the new emphasis the Catholic church wanted to place on the Marian cult to combat the theses of Luther's Reformation. The panel, from Sogliani's mature years, is a good example of the classical current which would remain faithful to the models of Raphael and Fra Bartolomeo even as Mannerism flourished.
Recent restorations have brought back the full chromatic range of this fine altarpiece.

32

32 - **Filippino Lippi** (Prato 1457-Florence 1504)
The Magdalene and St. John the Baptist. Inv. 1890 n° 8651 and 8653.
These were the two side panels of a tryptych. The central painting showed the Crucifix between the Virgin and St. Francis and was originally in the Valori chapel in the Church of S. Procolo in Florence. The dry and severe tones along with the hard and twisted lines make it likely that it was painted between 1497 and 1500 although the fact that it is in poor condition has affected the interpretation.

33 - **Perugino** (Pietro Vannucci, Citta della Pieve c. 1448-Fontignano 1523)
Filippino Lippi (Prato 1457-Florence 1504)
Deposition. Inv. 1890 n° 8370.
Work on the altarpiece, which was begun by Filippino Lippi who did the top part (Christ taken down from the Cross) was interrupted when the artist died in 1504 and it was completed by Perugino who may have been helped by the young Raphael (perhaps on the figure of the Magdalene). It was part of a large, four-sided altar in the center of the main chapel in the church of SS. Annunziata, and faced the congregation. The other sides were decorated with panels of different shapes and sizes which can be seen in other museums in Italy and abroad since it was dismantled starting in 1546 when the two main panels were replaced by a large wooden ciborium.
Lengthy recent restorations and careful studies have made it possi-

33

ble to clarify the history of this painting and to distinguish the parts done by the two artists. It is outstanding for its comprehension of Florentine painting between the fifteenth and sixteenth centuries.

34 - **Perugino** (Pietro Vannucci, Città della Pieve c. 1448-Fontignano 1523)
Assumption of the Virgin. Inv. 1890 n° 8366.
On 8 July 1500 this panel painting was placed on the high altar of the church of the Vallombrosa monastery near Florence, and from there it was moved to the Accademia when the monastery was shut down in 1810. Originally it was in an elaborate frame with a predella, that included two portraits of Vallombrosian monks which are now in the Uffizi Gallery.
The altarpiece follows a scheme that Perugino had used with

34

great success and a fine technique that has allowed the intensity of the colore to come down to us nearly intact.

35 - **Andrea del Sarto** (Florence 1486-1530)
Pietà. Inv. 1890 n° 8675.
The original of this fresco was in the novitiate of the convent of SS Annunziata where Vasari said that it "was in a niche at the top of the stairs". It was removed in 1810 and taken to the Accademia. Painted sometime between 1514 and 1525, although scraped and

35

damaged, this painting still has exquisitely intense colors and conveys great spiritual feeling.

36

36 - **Fra Bartolomeo** (Bartolomeo di Paolo del Fattorino, Savignano di Prato 1472 Florence 1517)
Job. Inv. 1890 n° 1449.
This panel and its companion piece portraying the prophet Isaiah flanked the painting of Christ as Salvator Mundi and the Four Evangelists (currently in the Pitti Palace); they were commissioned by Salvatore Billi to decorate the family chapel in the church of SS Annunziata.
The central portion is dated 1516, but the two side panels were done a year or two earlier immediately after Fra Bartolomeo's trip to Rome. In fact, there is a clear relationship with Michelangelo's frescoes in the Sistine Chapel.

The Musical Instruments

The Colossus room now contains a temporary display of the most important musical instruments in the historic collection of the Conservatorio Statale Luigi Cherubini. According to the provisions of an agreement, all the musical instruments that belong to this prestigious Florentine institute have been given to the Accademia Gallery on loan, while awaiting the establishment of a dedicated museum.
Twenty-three of the twenty-five instruments currently on display (February 1998), are behind glass. As soon as the new rooms are ready, presumably in 1999, they will be moved to their permanent new homes. We hope that in the near future visitors will be able to see the items described here in the Museum of Musical Instruments of the Conservatorio Cherubini. Access to the new museum will be via the Gallery entrance, with separate tickets.
The most significant core of the collection is a group of nine string instruments and a psaltery that belonged to the Medici, specifically, the grand duke Ferdinando (1663 - 1773). Five of the instruments on display in the Accademia Gallery belonged to his personal collection.
There are some keyboard instruments datable prior to the widespread use of the piano, the history of which is well documented by the pieces on display.
Currently, following some acquisitions and donations (the latest is the Gatti Kraus Collection received from Canada in the summer of 1997) the Cherubini collection comprises over two hundred instruments, many of which are quite outstanding.

37 - **Antonio Stradivarius** (Cremona? 1644-ivi? 1737)
Viola (known as the "Medici) *and Violoncello.*
These two antique instruments are among the most famous in the world. They were made by Antonio Stradivarius in 1690 for the grand duke Ferdinando de' Medici. Originally, they were part of a quintet that consisted of another violin (which is conserved in the Accademia di Santa Cecilia in Rome) and an alto viola. The tenor viola (generally known as the Medici Viola) is the only Stradivarius instrument that is completely intact with all its orig-

37

inal parts.
Antonio Stradivarius was the founder and most outstanding member of the great family of violin makers - their instruments are known for their remarkable sound quality.

38

38 - Bartolomeo Cristofori
(Padua 1655-Florence 1832)
Double Bass.
This instrument, from the grand duke's court, initially had four strings, and it was brought to the institute in its original form. The parts that were replaced including the neck have been lost. Bartolomeo Cristofori is known mainly for having invented the piano (or rather, as he originally defined it the "gravecembalo with piano and forte" by replacing the harpsichord's saltarello that picked at the cords in the same manner, with the modern hammers that permit dynamic variations to create the "piano" - soft and "forte" - loud sounds).
His position as the conservator of musical instruments at the Medici court was later extended to violin maker as we can see from the large, and complex instrument.

39 - Unknown Craftsman
Marble Psaltery.
Inside the wooden casing, we can see the Medici coat of arms and the following inscription:

> *al tosco gran signor volgi tue piante*
> *meraviglia è di lui marmo suonante*
> *cosi parlommi al cuor la sorte amica*
> *cosi beningo il ciel par che mi dica*

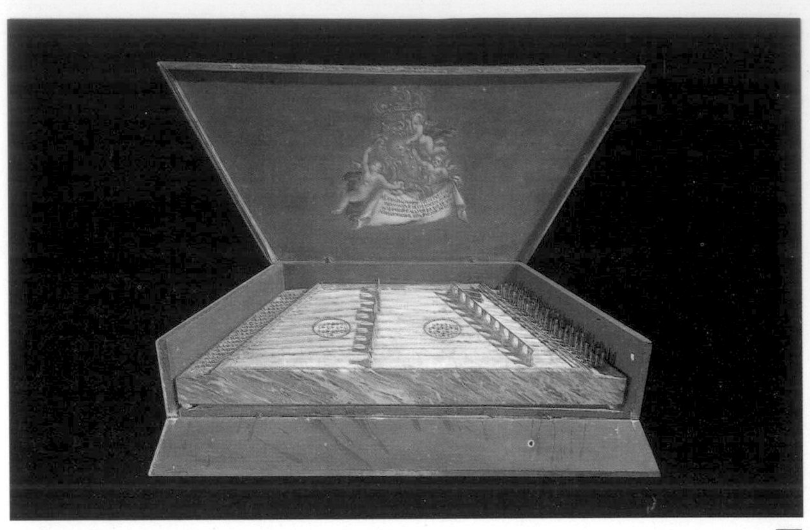

39

This rare specimen, is the only one in the world made of this material.

40 - **Bartolomeo Cristofori** (Padua 1655-Florence 1732)
Piano keyboard.
Three of Bartolomeo Cristofori's pianos have survived to the present:
- *1720 Hammerklavier, Metropolitan Museum of Art, New York*
- *1822 Piano, Museo degli Strumenti Musicali, Rome*
- *1726 Grand piano, Musikinstrumenteenmuseum, Karl Marx University, Leipzig.*

40

The keyboard on display here, datable around 1725, comes from the Gatti Kraus collection that was recently donated to the Conservatorio Cherubini. Although many parts have been replaced or restored, it is a fundamental link in the history of the piano.

41 - **Domenico del Mela** (Galliano nel Mugello, first half of XVIII cent.)
Upright piano.

Domenico del Mela was the first to develop and build this type of instrument. There is no biographical information about him, other than his birthplace.
This piano, one of the most famous and interesting items in the Florentine collection was transferred to the Museo Cherubini in 1928 after it had been purchased by the Del Mela Family.
There are forty-five keys, twenty-seven of carved yellow wood and eighteen black. A wooden bar in front of the keyboard bears the inscription: P. Dominicus del Mela de Galiano inventor fecit anno MDCCXXXIX.
The two articulated handles on the side make it possible to separate the instrument from the base.

41

42 - Seven models of antique and relatively modern piano mechanisms trace the origins and development of the instrument. They were built in 1876 by Cesare Ponsicchi, the piano tuner and restorer of the Regio Istituto Musicale

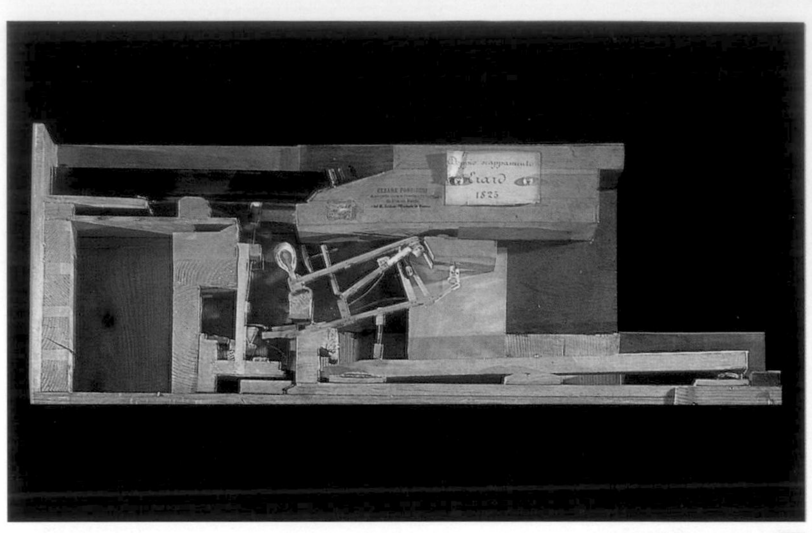

(Model n. 1) **42**

of Florence, to celebrate the two-hundred-twenty-fifth anniversary of the birth of Bartolomeo Cristofori, inventor of the piano.

Model n. 1 - The first model invented by Cristofori and described by Marchese Scipione Maffei in 1711 in the *Giornale dei letterati d'Italia*.

Model n. 2 - The second, perfected model by Cristofori. The windchest is not inverted as it is in the 1720 instrument which is in the Metropolitan Museum of Art in New York.

Model n. 3 - Model of hammer mechanism by Marius, 1716.

Model n. 4 - Model of hammer mechanism by Schroeter, 1721.

Model n. 5 - Model of a perfected Viennese mechanism.

Model n. 6 - Model of a perfected English mechanism. Pleyel System.

Model n. 7 - Model of a perfected, double Erard mechanism.

Lateral Wings of the Tribune

Here are several paintings - some of extraordinary size - done by artists who were either Michelangelo's contemporaries, or who came shortly after him. The relatively recent setting, which replaces a series of tapestries that have been removed for restoration, helps the visitor fit the David and Michelangelo's other sculptures into the historical context. In addition to highlighting his genius, it helps discover the deeper roots in contact with the Florentine Renaissance.
To learn more about sixteenth century painting in Florence: Uffizi Gallery, Palatine Gallery, Monumental Apartments in Palazzo Vecchio.

43 - **Francesco Granacci** (Villamagna 1469-Florence 1543)
The Martyrdom of Sta Apollonia. Inv. 1890 n° 8690.
Along with five others, this panel was part of the grand and complex altarpiece for the high altar of the church of the convent of Sta Apollonia in Florence. Many other artworks from this church can be seen in museums throughout Italy and abroad. According to Vasari, Michelangelo himself provided the general outline for the project, but there are no traces of these studies among the master's surviving drawings. The altarpiece, which on the basis of its style, can be dated around 1530 was dismantled between the end of the sixteenth and the beginning of the seventeenth

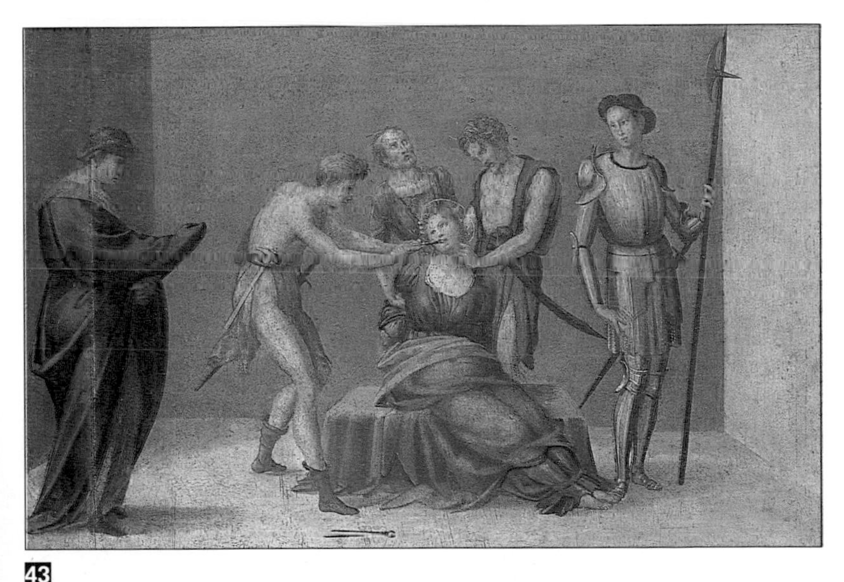

43

44

centuries to make room for a ciborium as required by the new rules imposed by the Counter Reformation.

44 - **Giuliano Bugiardini** (Florence 1476-1555)
Madonna with Jesus and St. Giovannino. Inv. 1890 n° 3121.
Signed and dated 1520, this is one of the few artworks that did not enter the Accademia collections as a result of the closing of convents and monasteries, It was purchased from the private collection of Villa Mansi, near Lucca. In this painting Bugiardini, who was usually close to Fra Bartolomeo and Mariotto Albertinelli in terms of style, seems to display a certain affinity

45

with Raphael's mature works (the composition as a whole is based on the Esterhazy Madonna) that Bugiardini saw during a trip to Rome between 1518 and 1519.

45 - **Bronzino** (Agnolo di Cosimo Tori, Florence 1503-1572)
Deposition. Inv. 1890 n° 3491.
The painting, which comes from the church of the Frati Minori Osservanti of Portoferraio was ordered by the Grand Duke Cosimo I de' Medici. It was damaged in 1817 by incorrect cleaning and it was decided to move it to the Uffizi Gallery in Florence from where it was later transferred to the Accademia. A letter

46

from the grand duke to Bronzino tells us that the painting arrived at Pisa in 1565 to be forwarded by sea to Leghorn and therefore, that year is the antequem for the painting which is from the master's late, and rather tired period. The chronology is also confirmed by Bronzino's self-portrait in the background on the left, showing him as an old man.

46 - **Alessandro Allori** (Florence 1535-1607)
Annunciation. Inv. 1890 n° 494.
This painting, on which the date 1603 is clearly visible was in the Medici villa of Castello (near Florence) until 1799. Its small size and warm tone of the composition, with the Virgin who seems to want to flee from the angel in her room leads us to believe that the painting was originally meant for a private setting, rather than a place of worship.
This hypothesis is also borne out by the stupendous still-life in the lower left, which is almost a picture within the picture. The

47

observer's attention is drawn more to the still life with its austere and profound beauty than to the Gospel scene.

47 - **Pontormo** (Jacopo Carrucci, Pontorme 1494-Florence 1556)
Venus and Cupid. Inv. 1890 n° 1570.
This painting from the Medici collections reached the Accademia in 1850. It was immediately restored and the robes that had been painted over Venus to hide her nakedness shortly after the painting was completed were removed. Pontormo did this painting around the mid-fifteen forties for Bartolomeo Bettini to a cartoon

TOMMASO MANZUOLI
DETTO MASO DA S. FRIANO
LA TRINITÀ E VARI SANTI

48

by Michelangelo. Buonarotti's hand is evident in the majestic and articulated nude Venus, while the landscape and the unsettling still life in the background are more similar to Pontormo's personal style.

Left wing

48 - **Maso da San Friano** (Tommaso Manzuoli, Florence c. 1531-1571)
Trinity and Saints. Inv. 1890 n° 2118.
The painting came to the Accademia from the Chamber of Commerce sometime in 1777. It had been commissioned by the leather guild, as confirmed by the presence of St. Crispin, its patron saint (in the back and to the right). The style is characterized by fidelity to Rosso Fiorentino's Mannerism: elongated and softly faceted shapes, in sharp yet slightly unfocused colors. These observations lead critics to believe that he had already lost touch with Pontormo, Foschi and Andrea del Sarto and that it was painted during his last decade of work.

49 - **Alessandro Allori** (Florence 1535-1607)
Coronation of the Virgin. Inv. 1890 n° 3171.
This awe-inspiring painting was done in 1593 for the main altar of the church of Santa Maria degli Angioli in Florence. It is a particularly impressive composition done late in Allori's life. The painter was also the master of Agnolo Bronzino. The tall vase of flowers in the foreground, a true still-life is one of the most striking features, it fits perfectly with the semi-precious stone inlays that the grand ducal factory made starting in that period to decorate ebony cabinets and tables.

50 - **Cosimo Gamberucci** (Florence c. 1560-1621)
St. Peter Healing the Cripple. Inv. 1890 n° 4631.
The picture, dated 1599, adorned the Miglioritti family's altar in the church of S. Pier Maggiore (Florence) where it remained until the building was destroyed in 1783. Gamberucci is one of those seventeenth century Florentine painters whose image and talents were only recently rediscovered by the critics. His background is linked basically to Santi di Tito and he remained royal to his teachings throughout most of his career. This painting, however, includes bright colors, in the manner of Cigoli and a search for a new narrative style taken from the example of Empoli.

49

50

51 - **Carlo Portelli** (Loro Ciuffenna?-Florence 1574)
Dispute over the Immaculate Conception. Inv. 1890 n° 4630.
This painting, signed and dated 1566, comes from the church of Ognissanti where it was replaced, in 1671, by another on the same theme by Vincenzo Dandini. Portelli, a pupil of Ridolfo del Ghirlandaio and, in turn, teacher of Maso da San Friano, displayed the full repertory of forms and postures that were typical of his eclectic Mannerist style. The subject, which can also be seen in a painting by Sogliani (in the Colossus room) was a

51

favorite of the Counter-Reformation when the Roman Catholic Church was intent on glorifying the figure of the Virgin May.

52 - **Santi di Tito** (Sansepolcro 1536-Florence 1603)
The Entry into Jerusalem. Inv. 1890 n° 8667.
This grand composition comes from the church of Monteoliveto near Florence and can be dated between 1569 and 1579. The preparatory drawing is in Stuttgart. Alongside of the clear and well structured figures, typical of all his paintings, Santi di Tito

52

leaned towards a crowded, animated effect which is balanced by the tranquility of the classical landscape in the background. It is aufficient to compare this painting with Portelli's Dispute Over the Immaculate Conception to grasp the balance and spontaneity of Santi di Tito's work as compared to his Mannerist contemporaries.

53

The Gallery of the Plaster Models

Since 1985 this gallery, also known as the "Salone delle Toscane" or Gallery of the Tuscans, has housed the collection of original plaster models by two nineteenth century Tuscan sculptors, Lorenzo Bartolini and Luigi Pampaloni.
Along with the statues, there are also paintings by former students of the Accademia who went on to achieve fame (Silvestro Lega, Luigi Mussini, and others). This room is a deliberate reference to the Gallery's origins and its unbreakable ties to the art school.
The many portrait busts present a varied and fascinating overview of the nineteenth century bourgeoisie and nobility. Bartolini and Pampaloni were not admired only in Italy, they both had a large clientele in France, England and Poland.
The dark spots on the surfaces of nearly all the plaster casts were the references the artists used to transfer the shapes and sizes from the model to the marble sculpture.
To learn more about nineteenth century painting and sculpture in Florence: Gallery of Modern Art, Palazzo Pitti, and the Church of Santa Croce.

53 - **Luigi Mussini** (Berlin 1813-Siena 1888)
Sacred Music. Inv. Accademia n° 292.
The painting was done in Rome in 1841 and was put on display at the Accademia in the same year until 1867 when it was moved to the Gallery of Modern Art. It is a major example of the Tuscan purist school which comprised the return to fifteenth century Umbrian styles typical of the "Nazarenes" and the rigor of Ingres whom Mussini had known personally.

54 - **Lorenzo Bartolini** (Savignano di Prato 1777-Florence 1850)
The Campbell Sisters. Inv. Sculptures n° 1183.
The group portrays Emma and Julia Campbell children of Lady Charlotte Campbell (youngest daughter of the Duke of Argyll) who came to Florence between September 1819 and August 1820 to write a book. Bartolini carved the statue during that period and sent it to the family castle in Scotland where it can still be seen today. It is one of the artist's mature works, and follows classic examples, reflecting the harmony and balance along with the grace transmitted by Canova.

54 55

55 - **Lorenzo Bartolini** (Savignano di Prato 1777-Florence 1850)
The Winepresser. Inv. Sculptures n° 1216.
This statue, which has several names in Italian (L'ammostatore, Il vendemmiatore, Il pigiatore di uva and Il Bacchino) was done around 1818 for the French collector, Count de Pourtales and sent to Paris. Bartolini's second version of the statue was delivered to Count Tosi di Brescia in 1844 and is currently in the Pinacoteca Tosi Martinengo. There are several copies by other artists; the statue achieved its fame because of the neofifteenth century features inspired by grace and purity of form, as well as the moral significance of this figure who is so dedicated to and confident of the value of his work.

56 - **Pontormo** (Jacopo Carrucci, Pontorme 1494-Florence 1557)
The Women's Ward in the Hospital of S. Matteo. Inv. 1890 n° 9385.
This fresco is now back in its original place after having been removed for restorations. It shows the women's ward in the hospital of S. Matteo which is what this room was in the early sixteenth century. The painting may have been an ex voto ordered by a patient; it is dated around 1514 because of stylistic similarities with other works from the period and its importance lies in the portrayal of an important yet relatively unknown aspect of

56

Florentine life in the Renaissance. The three-color technique that used only pink, yellow and green to create a bas-relief or stucco decoration effect is also quite unusual.

57 - **Lorenzo Bartolini** (Savignano di Prato 1777-Florence 1850)
Portrait of Franz Liszt. Inv. Sculptures n° 1467. Bartolini sculpted the bust during a Florentine sojourn between 1838 and 1839 along with his friend Madame d'Agoult (who wrote under the pen-name of Daniel Stern); the plaster model is next to the bust of Liszt. Portraiture took up a great deal of Bartolini's time and played a fundamental role in the creation of his international reputation. The large number of plaster models on display provides a good understanding of how, along with fine quality busts that involved careful studies of the subjects as they penetrate their souls, Bartolini's workshop turned out more or less series works, with but few variations, to satisfy the demands of the emerging bourgeoisie.

57

58

58 - **Lorenzo Bartolini** (Savignano di Prato 1777-Florence 1850)
The Vow of Innocence. Inv. Sculptures n° 1211.
This statue of a young giri, also known as l'Insensibile was done in 1848 for the prince of Sant'Antimo of Naples; it fits into the didactic illustrative context so dear to Romantic tastes. To quote the sculptor's words, it portrays "...Innocence about to take the vow of Chastity, as she offers up two turtledoves..." with an intrinsic lesson in morality.

59

59 - **Lorenzo Bartolini** (Savignano di Prato 1777-Florence 1850) *Monument to Niccolò Demidoff.* Inv. Sculptures n° 1174-1177, 1209, 1221.
The marble grouping stands in Piazza Demidoff (Florence) adjacent to Lungarno Serristori in the S. Niccolò district. Only part of the plaster models are here in the Accademia: the central group (the model was lost) shows Count Demidoff, private advisor and chamberlain to the Zar, with his son Anatoli and Gratitude at his

60

side; the four lateral groups portray Mercy, Siberia with the young god Pluto, a Muse and Truth revealing herself to Art. The monument, ordered by Pavel and Anatoli upon their father's death in 1828, was supposed to have been completed in 1833, but was only unveiled in 1871 many years after the artist had died. It was completed by Bartolini's pupil Pasquale Romanelli.

60 - **Luigi Pampaloni** (Florence 1791-1847)
Girl with a Turtle Dove. Inv. Sculptures n° 1236.
In 1831 Pampaloni exhibited this sculpture in the triennial competition of the Accademia where he taught. We do not know whether he showed the plaster model or the finished marble

61

sculpture. It was immediately praised, and the *Gazzetta di Firenze* wrote "graceful and gentle beyond words", emphasized its naturalness, a feature that was particularly dear to the Romantic tastes, In fact, Pampaloni repeated this sweet image several times for various clients and even today, it is one of the most widely used themes for small, decorative sculptures.

61 - **Luigi Pampaloni** (Florence 1791-1847)
Filippo Brunelleschi. Inv. Sculptures n° 1231.
The plaster model, made in 1828, is part of a group that the artist's widow donated to the Accademia immediately after his death, but was only put on display in 1883. The marble statue

was placed in the niche in the clergy's residence in Piazza del Duomo where it stili stands with its companion statue of Arnolfo di Lapo. This sculpture acquired considerable fame for Pampaloni: it was admired by Thorwaldsen and the grand duke himself sponsored his election to the Royal Academy of Florence in 1830.

62 - **Lorenzo Bartolini** (Savignano di Prato 1777-Florence 1850)
Love, Vice and Wisdom. Inv. Sculptures n° 1220.
This is the original plaster model of the high-relief marble panel made for Prince Demidoff. It is also known as "The Sleep of Hapless Virtue and Luxurious Opulence" or "The Panel of the Cupids". In 1845 Bartolini described the complex subject as follows "The God of Love of the generation reclines over the world and watches over the symbolic genie of unbridled wealth without virtue, snoring in the relaxed sleep of the revelers and lovers, tousled hair, cup overturned...Abandoned unto himself he sleeps the restless sleep of misfortune and of the glory of the Genie of the ambitious righteousness of work and serves as a pillow for oppressive destiny, covered by the decency that gives knowledge...".

62

63 - **Lorenzo Bartolini** (Savignano di Prato 1777-Florence 1850)
Monument to Leon Battista Alberti. Inv. Sculptures n° 1180.
Work on this group was begun in 1838. It was ordered by Count Leon Battista Alberti, descendant of the famous Renaissance architect, for the church of Sta Croce in Florence where the marble version still stands today. Alberti is shown supported by an angel on either side, and the serpent of envy lies dead at his feet. The group, which was unveiled only a year after Bartolini's death is a fine example of a monument to an historical figure. The artist excelled in this genre (see the monument to Machiavelli. sculpted for the Uffizi Loggia) which, however, never fully revealed his finest talents that we remore suited to mythological and allegorical subjects or portraits.

64 - **Lorenzo Bartolini** (Savignano di Prato 1777-Florence 1850)
Countess Sofia Zamoyska. Inv. Sculptures n° 1314.
This plaster is a reproduction of the marble monument in the Salviati Chapel in the Church of Santa Croce, Florence. It was begun in 1837 on commission from Prince Stanislas Zamoyski of Warsaw and his children, in memory of the countess who died on 27 February of that year. Bartolini made the plaster model the year he received the commission, but the marble statue was only placed in the Florentine basilica in 1844. This sculpture is outstanding for the attention the artist dedicated to the fine decorative details on the antique bed, and the drapings of the clothes, the veil and thc sheets.

63

64

The Byzantine Rooms

The three rooms take their name from the fact that they contain works starting from the second half of the thirteenth century, the period when Florentine painting was dominated by Byzantine influences. Actually, only the center room contains works predating Giotto, while the others are dedicated to his followers. The recent rennovations of the of the rooms, was done according to the most rigid scientific criteria, reserved the right-side room to Giotto's helpers and direct disicples such as Taddeo Gaddi and Bernardo Daddi, and the one on the left to the group comprising Orcagna, Andrea, Nardo and Jacopo di Cione, the legitimate heirs to the most rigorous late forteenth century Giotto-esque tradtion. *To learn more about fourteenth century painting in Florence: Uffizi Gallery, Church of Santa Croce.*

Center Room

65 - **Maestro di S. Gaggio** (Florence, late XIII-early XIV cent.) *Madonna Enthroned with Child and Saints.* Inv. 1890 n° 6115.

The painting comes trom the S. Gaggio monastery in Florence, and it is from there that the artist (perhaps Grifo di Tancredi who probably studied in the workshop of the Maestro della Maddalena, or close to that environment) gets his name. An intelligent interpreter of the innovations created by Cimabue, the Maestro di S. Gaggio went on to interpret Giotto in a highly personal manner as can be seen from this early fourtheenth century painting. He adopted Giotto's sense of volume (see the face and neck of the Virgin) and complemented it with a very original and elegant use of color.

65

66 - **Maestro della Croce delle Oblate** (unknown artist from Lucca, first half of the XIII century)

Virgin Enthroned with Child and Two Angels. Inv. 1890 n° 433. This painting now reveals its terse, glazed colors following recent restorations that have highlighted the exquisite workmanship and the minute details on the decorations of the fabrics and clear outlines of the faces. The unknown artist, known as the "Maestro della Croce delle Oblate"- from his most famous work - was trained in Lucca, but undoubtedly had many contacts with the Florentine environment, and worked between 1230 and 1255. The painting, which was cut along the bottom edge is a significant example of the Byzantine style, from which the room gets its name.

66

67

67 - Maestro della Maddalena

(Florence, second half of the XIII cent.)

The Magdalene Repenting and Scenes from her Life. Inv. 1890 n° 8466.

Painted between 1265 and 1290 by an unknown artist who was head of one of the most active Florentine workshops, this panel comes from the Convent of the SS Annunziata. Early in his artistic development he was influenced by the Maestro del Bigallo and the Maestro di Rovezzano; later he was sensitive to innovations brought about by Coppo di Marcovaldo and Cimabue. This painting, datable in his mature period. between 1280 and 1285, is distinguished for its lively narrative which is particularly evident in the lateral scenes.

68

68 - **Pacino di Buonaguida** (Florence. data from 1303 to 1339)
The Tree of Life. Inv. 1890 n° 8459.
This painting, which was originally in the Convent of the Clarisse at Monticelli near Florence, it was moved to the convent in Via dei Malcontenti, then to the Pia Casa di Lavoro di Montedomini and finally reached the Accademia.
The painter illustrated the "Lignum vitae" which St. Bonaventure wrote in 1274. Many passages are transcribed on the scrolls and inscriptions: however there are also many Biblical verses so that as a whole the composition seems to be a page from a text that attracts the eyes with its delicately splendid colors. But its greater and true aim is that of being read with the mind and the spirit. In addition to being a skilled painter, Pacino was a fine miniaturist and illuminator: he probably worked on this major project between 1305 and 1310.

69 - **Pacino di Buonaguida** (Florence, data from 1303 to 1339)
St. Procolo, St. John the Evangelist, St. Nicholas. Inv. 1890 n° 8700, 8699, 8698.
These three panels come from the Badia Fiorentina, but since the property of the church of S. Procolo was moved there in 1778, it is likely that they were originally in the other building. In fact, old guides mention a polytypch in S. Procolo, with the Madonna in the center, flanked by Saints John the Baptist, John the Evangelist, Nicholas and Procolo.
In this painting, which can be dated around 1320/1330, Pacino di Buonaguida displays a strong sense of plasticity and form which confirm his rather prompt acceptance of Giotto's new style of painting.

9

70 - **Taddeo Gaddi** (Florence, data from 1327 to 1366)
Nativity Scene. Inv. 1890 n° 8583.
Stigmata of St. Francis. Inv. 1890 n° 8602.
Originally there were 26 panels and two semi lunettes (now in one single lunette) that decorated the cabinet of the reliquaries in the Basilica of Sta Croce in Florence. In 1810 when Napoleon ordered the closing of many religious institutions the panels were taken to the Accademia, and four were sold to private parties (two are currently in Berlin and two in Munich). Reconstruction of the cabinet has been difficult and controversial: according to one hypothesis, scenes from the life of Christ

70

were on the left, and those from the life of St. Francis on the right. Another theory holds that one group was visible when the cabinet was closed and the other when it was open. Certainly the aim was to emphasize the parallels between the lives of Christ and St. Francis, a concept that was fully illustrated in Medieval art.

Chronologically the work can be dated around 1333-1334. The style is clearly akin to Giotto's paintings in the Bardi chapel in Sta Croce, as regards the scenes of St. Francis, while the paintings of the Christ show greater artistic freedom and some influence from the Siena school. On the whole the panels document a very fruitful period in Gaddi's career in a free and sometimes even daring interpretation of his Florentine roots.

70

71 - **Bernardo Daddi** (Florence, data from 1312 to 1348)
Painted Cross. Inv. 1890 n° 442.

It is possible that this large Crucifix comes from the church of S. Donato in Polverosa near Florence and, like all similar crosses hung between the presbytery and the nave. The severe, subdued style (the structure is quite simple and, in fact, almost archaic), along with the minute and elegantly detailed scenes in the foils,

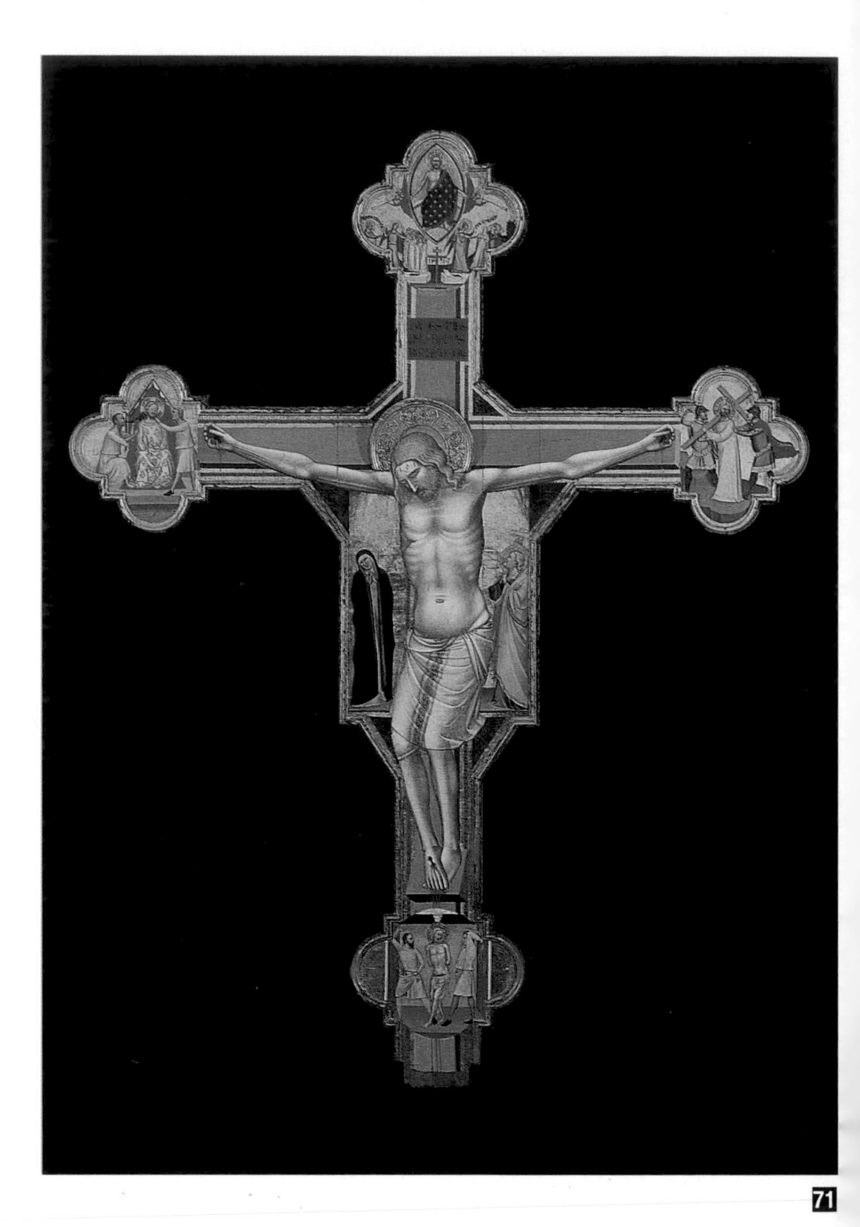

71

72

would suggest that it was painted towards the end of Daddi's career, a few years before the great plague of 1348 carried him off.

72 - **Bernardo Daddi** (Florence, data from 1312 to 1348)
Coronation of the Virgin. Inv. 1890 n° 3449.
This complex painting comes from the altar of S. Marco in the left transept of the church of Sta Maria Novella; it has also been called the Coronation of Our Lady. It is from Bernardo Daddi's later period, when his workshop had grown and accepted artists who would later go out and make names for themselves such as Puccio di Simone, whose hand can be seen in some parts of this polyptych.

73

73 - **Bernardo Daddi** (Florence, data from 1312 to 1348)
Crucifixion. Inv. 1890 n° 443.

Puccio di Simone (Florence, data from c. 1346 to 1358)
The Magdalene, the Archangel Michael, St. Julian, St. Martha. Inv. 1890 n° 6140.

The central part of this polyptych, depicting the Crucifixion has been attributed to the later part of Bernardo Daddi's career. It was separated from the lateral saints probably after it was removed from the church where it originally hung, perhaps even in the nineteenth century. In 1915 it was given to the Museo Civico of Pistoia where it stayed until 1981. The four lateral panels, were painted by Puccio di Simone, an artist who worked in Daddi's atelier, but with enough of a distinctive style that makes it possible to identify his works. They were given to the Conservatorio di Sant'Elisabetta in Barga (Lucca) for storage in 1932 and remained there until 1980. The recomposition, as we see it now is the result of recent studies

74

and adds data to our knowledge of the history of Bernardo Daddi's busy and diversified atelier, before the great plague of 1348 brought his life to an untimely end.

Left Room

74 - **Andrea Orcagna** (Andrea di Cione, Florence, data from 1343 to 1368) *Madonna Enthroned with Child and Saints*. Inv. 1890 n° 3469.
This painting comes from the church of SS. Annunziata, perhaps from the chapel of the Del Palagio family that was founded in 1353 and frescoed by Taddeo Gaddi with scenes from the life of St. Nicholas.
Although its style speaks for a date around 1355, it is not considered to have been done entirely by Orcagna, but rather by several of the very talented artists in his large and busy workshop.

75

75 - **Andrea Orcagna** (Andrea di Cione. Florence, data from 1343 to 1368)
Pentecost. Inv. Storage n° 165.
This painting. from the high altar of the church of SS Apostoli in Florence was moved to the Badia Fiorentina before 1771 the year in which it was restored by the Canon Bonsi. The features of its style qualify it as deriving from an idea by Andrea di Cione who probably drew it and began the painting. However, it seems that most of the work was done by an assistant or pupil who may have been Spinello Aretino. In that case, this would be one of his earliest attempts at painting during the period (1370-75) that he was still at Orcagna's workshop.

76 - **Jacopo di Cione** (Florence, data from 1365 to 1398)
Coronation of the Virgin. Inv. 1890 n° 456.
The officers of the Florentine Mint commissioned Simone and Niccolò and Jacopo Cini to do this painting in 1372. The style reflects the work of Jacopo di Cione, brother of Orcagna, and therefore, critics tend to regard the name "Cini" as a misspelling

of "Cioni". Niccolò and Simone, perhaps Niccolò di Pietro Gerini and Simone di Lapo Gucci do not seem to have had much of a hand in the painting given its overall homogeneity. Specific studies have analyzed the characteristics of the fine draping behind the figures and recognized similarities with other paintings from the same workshop.

77 - **Jacopo di Cione** (Florence, data from 1365 to 1398)
Crucifixion. Inv. 1890 n° 1670.
This painting reveals all the features of Orcagna's atelier, in the technique with which the colors were applied, thick and compact so that they resisted time and overpainting at later dates (the overpainting was eliminated by a modern restoration) and in the style itself, that is clearly based on Giotto, as we can see from the compact figures.
It had long been attributed to Niccolò di Pietro Gerini and his workshop, but now it is generally accepted as having been done by Jacopo di Cione.

78 - **Nardo di Cione** (Florence, data from c. 1343 to 1366)
The Trinity and Saints Romuald and John the Evangelist. Inv. 189(
n° 8464.
Giovanni Ghiberti ordered this painting in 1365 for his chapel ir
the church of Sta Maria degli Angeli. Around 1750 it was movec
to the Della Stufa chapel dedicated to St. Andrew and the figur

79

of the Evangelist was modified accordingly. The painting has since been restored to its original appearance. Critics consider it stylistically close to Nardo di Cione, but it can be attributed to his workshop where other talented painters, including his brother Jacopo, worked with the master. And perhaps it was his brother's hand that painted the scenes on the predella.

79 - **Maestro della Cappella Rinuccini** (Florence, data from 1350 to c. 1380)
The Vision of St Bernard with Saints Benedict, John the Evangelist, Quintino and Galgano. Inv. 1890 n° 8463.
This painting was brought to the Accademia from the Badia Fiorentina which was probably not its original "home". It was painted by the anonymous pupil of Andrea Orcagna who worked on the Rinuccini Chapel in Sta Croce with Giovanni da Milano and completed it upon Giovanni's departure from Florence. His style combines the somewhat rigid monumentality of Orcagna's workshop with a richer decorative and color repertory derived from his relationship with Giovanni da Milano.

The First Floor Rooms

These rooms contain a practically unique collection of fourteenth and early fifteenth century Florentine panels on gold. There is a fine selection of post-Giotto painting trends, from Orcagna's workshop with its return to archaic forms, to Lorenzo Monaco's school (with 8 paintings by the master spanning his entire stylistic development), that is, those painters who started from the period of greatest sensitivity to the use of color and decorative effects in the Giottesque manner and were to flourish in the International Gothic style.
One of the outstanding figures is Lorenzo Monaco, whose paintings are represented here by a series of masterpieces that cover the entire time frame and style of his works.

80 - **Giovanni da Milano** (data from 1346 to 1369)
Pietà. Inv. 1890 n° 8467.
This painting, which comes from the monastery of S. Girolamo on the Costa S. Giorgio, bears the Strozzi and Rinieri coats of arms on the base of the lateral pillars. The inscription at the bottom gives the artist's name, Giovanni da Milano, and the date 1365, which makes it contemporary with the frescoes in the Rinuccini chapel in Sta Croce, Giovanni da Milano conveys intense feeling through the use of warm, soft colors which emphasize the movement of the Magdalene's long blond hair, and shade the broken forms of Christ's arms. The emotions, however, are intellectualistically encompassed by the pained but peaceful facial expressions and the balanced construction so that the painting can be considered a supreme culmination of Giottesque realism and northern sensitivity.

80

81

81 - Andrea di Bonajuto (data from 1343 to 1377)
Saint Agnes and Saint Domitilla. Inv. 1890 n° 3145.
These two paintings come from the hospital of Sta Maria Nuova in Florence and are excellent examples of Andrea's style around 1365, that is about when he did the frescoes in the monastery of Sta Maria Novella. The period more less followed his training with Nardo di Cione, when he had had an opportunity to assimilate the intensity of color from Giovanni da Milano. This diptych is distinguished by rich ornamentation and the courtly delicacy of the two figures.

82

82 - **Giovanni del Biondo** (Florence, data from 1356 to 1399)
Presentation in the Temple. Inv. 1890 n° 8462.
The tryptych was originally in the chapter room of the Florentine convent of Sta Maria degli Angioli. and is dated 1364. The artist, generally recognized as Giovanni del Biondo. was a member of Orcagna's circle as evidenced by the rigidly schematic figures. However, his style is distinct from that of other members of the group due to his attention to Sienese trends as shown by the brighter and glossier colors and the details painted with devoted care.

83 - **Giovanni del Biondo** (Florence, data from 1356 to 1399)
Annunciation. Inv. 1890 n° 8606.
The large polyptych can be dated around 1380. It comes from the Cavalcanti chapel in Sta Maria Novella that was built by Monna Andreola in suffrage of her husband's soul, Mainardo Cavalcanti who died in 1379. This large structure, complete with predella,

3

84

pinnacles and columns gives a complete, realistic idea of what a fourteenth century ancona was like including the solid, elegant engraved and gilded wooden structure.

84 - **Mariotto di Nardo** (Florence, data from 1394 to 1424)
Madonna and Child with Saints. Inv. 1890 n° 8612, 8613, 3258-3260
This tryptych was ordered by the Corsini family for the church of S. Gaggio. There is general agreement that it was done by Mariotto di Nardo and it can be dated between 1390 and 1395 due to the similarities with the large altarpiece in the church of S. Domenico at Villamagna which was documented as having been done in 1394-1395.

35

35 - **Niccolò di Pietro Gerini** (Florence, data from 1368 to 1415)
Spinello Aretino (Arezzo c. 1350-1411)
Lorenzo di Niccolò (Florence 1376-1440)
Coronation of the Virgin. Inv. 1890 n° 8468.
The polyptych dated 1401 was commissioned by Lorenza de' Mozzi, abbess of the convent of Sta Felicita in 1395 for the church's main altar. It was only begun in 1399 by the three painters who worked on it together, as was often customary in that period. Critics, however, cannot agree on attributing any specific parts of the work to the individual artists so there are many theories in circulation.

86 - **Spinello Aretino** (Arezzo 1350 c.-1411)
Virgin and Child with Saints. Inv. 1890 n° 8461.
This panel comes from the church of Sant'Andrea in Lucca, and is clear evidence that this painter, born in Arezzo, but trained in Florence also worked in other artistically important Tuscan cities. He was in close contact with Orcagna's atelier and also worked on the Palazzo Pubblico in Siena. The inscription with the date 1391 is neither complete nor original, but its contents are reliable because the features of the painting correspond to that stylistic period when the artist was still dependent on Orcagna's teaching: the rounded shapes of the figures and the severe and limited chromatic range.

87 - **Niccolò di Pietro Gerini** (Florence, data from 1369 to 1415)
Pietà. Inv. 1890 n° 5048, 5066, 5067.
The painting comes from the church of Sta Maria Novella where it had been hung from the first pillar one sees leaving the Sacristy. As the inscription under the figure of Christ reads, it belonged to the 'Compagnia dei disciplinati del Pellegrino". Some of the members are portrayed in the cuspid and predella wearing the typical hooded garments that allowed them to perform acts of charity

87

without being recognized in accordance with the Evangelical spirit. The style of the painting places it in the latter period, between 1404 and 1408, of Niccolò di Pietro Gerini's work.

88 - **Niccolò di Pietro Gerini** (Florence, data from 1368 to 1415)
Crucifixion and Saints. Inv. 1890 n° 3152.
This painting, which can be dated around 1400, the latter part of Niccolò's career has some interesting iconographic and historical features. The figures on the center panel are smaller than the saints on the sides, which is curious but not unique in fourteenth and fifteenth century panel paintings, as we can see in the Crucifixion and Saints by Bernardo Daddi and Puccio Simone, in the Byzantine Rooms of the Gallery. In addition, the polyptych is surmounted by a later, fifteenth century addition in which Angolo di Domenico del Mazziere, a Florentine painter from Ghirlandaio's

88

circle portrayed the four Evangelists. In the Renaissance this device was used to give paintings a more modern, that is square, shape, by eliminating the cusps of the by then outmoded Gothic style.

89 - **Giovanni dal Ponte** (Giovanni di Marco, Florence 1385-1437) *Coronation of the Virgin*. Inv. 1890 n° 458.
This grand tryptych comes from the Ufficio del Monte di Pietà and can be dated around 1420. Giovanni di Marco, known as Del Ponte was a Florentine artist and pupil of Spinello Aretino. This talented, but not brilliant painter displays considerable sensitivity to the changing trends that swept through Florence during the early decades of the fifteenth century. Here, next to the sweet Gothic harmony of the Virgin, he reveals careful attention to Masaccio's innovations in the lateral saints, and in particular, the one on the right.

89

90

90 - **Rossello di Jacopo Franchi** (Florence 1377-1456)
Coronation of the Virgin. Inv. 1890 n° 8460.
This is a grandiose polyptych, rich in figures and ornaments, made for the Benedictine monastery at Le Campora near Florence. The date on the inscription is usually taken as 1420, however, since it was painted over during the last century it may have been 1422 the year in which the altar on which it stood was established. This richly decorated painting, with its crowded spaces and delicate, slim figures abundantly clothed in flowing robes is still clearly part of the Gothic world.

91

91 Agnolo Gaddi (Florence, data from 1369 to 1396)
Madonna of Humility. Inv. 1890 n° 461.
The painting, which comes from the convent of Sta Verdiana in Florence is generally attributed to the latter part of Agnolo Gaddi's career, that is when the master, son and heir to Taddeo's workshop, and pupil of Giotto revealed that he had absorbed the International, courtly and florid Gothic style brought to Florence by Simone Martini and the Maestro del Codice di S. Giorgio. The iconography of this Madonna, seated on the cushion on the ground was particulary popular in that school.

92 - **Lorenzo Monaco** (Piero di Giovanni, Siena? c. 1370 - Florence c. 1423-24)

Praying in the Garden. Inv. 1890 n° 438.

This painting, from the convent of the Angeli is considered to date from Lorenzo Monaco's early period when, alongside of elegant and fully Gothic linearity and the subtle, incisive brushstrokes of a miniaturist, which are unmistakable features of his work, there is a solid sense of volume and austere, archaic tension typical of the late XIV century Florentine environment following in the traces of Giotto's style as it was developed in the workshop of the Orcagna brothers.

93 - **Lorenzo Monaco** (Piero di Giovanni, Siena? c. 1370 - Florence c. 1423-24)

Pietà. Inv. 1890 n° 467.

Although we do not know where this painting originally hung, it is certain that it is one of Lorenzo Monaco's earlier works, perhaps done shortly after the Praying in the Garden The inscription

92

93

reads 1404, a date which is also confirmed by the accentuated Gothic lines (see the flowing folds in St. John's robes) and the refined elegance of the decorative details. Critics have recently recognized the hand of a member of the workshop in the upper portion of the painting.

94 - **Lorenzo Monaco** (Piero di Giovanni, Siena? c. 1370 - Florence c. 1423-24)
Painted Cross. Inv. 1890 n° 3153.
This crucifix, from the hospital of Sta Maria Nuova is the oldest in a series of similar pieces by Lorenzo Monaco and his workshop. Chronologically and stylistically it can be placed between the Pietà with the symbols of the Passion (1404) and the Madonna and Child with Saints from Monteoliveto (1407-1410) both of which are in the Accademia. The ornamental motifs impressed in gold are taken from the Pietà, although the Crucifix creates a richer effect since they are plaster reliefs, whereas the saints in the second painting are closer to the structure of the Christ.

94

95 - **Lorenzo Monaco** (Piero di Giovanni, Siena? c. 1370 - Florence c. 1423-24)

Virgin and Child with Saints. Inv. 1890 n° 470.

This painting, which came to the Florentine Gallery from a private collection and hence uncertain origins, has an inscription stating that it was done by Cennino Cennini in 1408. Actually, it has nothing to do with the modest painter who wrote the famous treatise on fourteenth century artistic techniques, it was definitely done by Lorenzo Monaco in his later years. The frame, and hence the inscription are false, and probably were added when the painting was acquired by the Toscanelli family.

95

96 - **Lorenzo Monaco** (Piero di Giovanni, Siena? c. 1370 - Florence c. 1423-24)

Madonna Enthroned with child and Saints. Inv. 1890 n° 468.

Brother Giovanni Istrada ordered this large polyptych for the Monteoliveto Monastery near Florence. According to the inscription beneath the central panel it was finished in 1410. Therefore, it is one of the painter's mature works, completed when the Gothic style was flourishing in Florence, as demonstrated by the fluid lines of the robes, the soft and harmoniously curving shapes, and the delicate, elegant illuminated figures on the pinnacles.

96

97 - **Lorenzo Monaco** (Piero di Giovanni, Siena? c. 1370 - Florence c. 1423-24)

The Virgin, Christ Crucified, St. John the Evangelist. Inv. 1890 n° 2169, 2141, 2140.

Originally these three paintings were to have been the cuspide of an altarpiece in the church of S. Jacopo sopr'Arno in Florence. Vasari described it, but by the last century it no longer existed. We can assume that it was destroyed in the XVIII century which is when the three small paintings were placed in carved and gilded Rococo frames. Although they have traditionally been attributed to Lorenzo Monaco, contemporary scholars say that they could have been done in the master's workshop to his own drawing sometime around 1415 as suggested by a stylistic comparison with other paintings from that period.

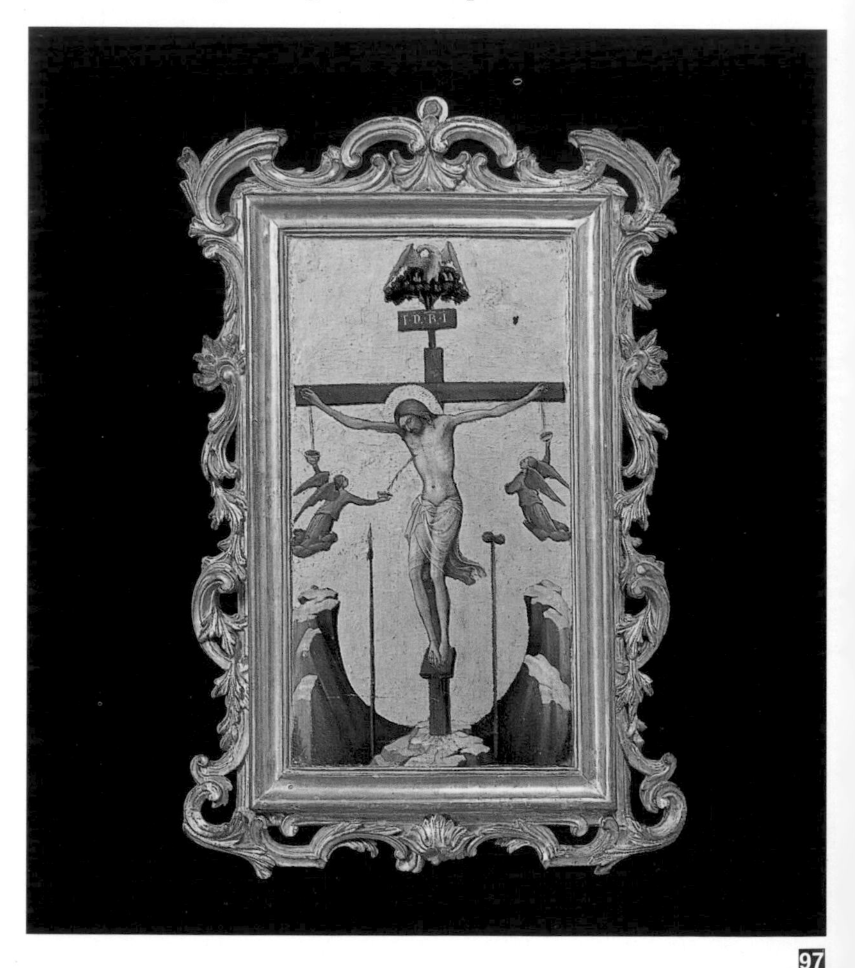

97

97

98 - **Lorenzo Monaco** (Piero di Giovanni, Siena? c. 1370 - Florence c. 1423-24)

Annunciation and Saints. Inv. 1890 n° 8458.

The tryptych from the Badia Fiorentina can be dated around 1418. It is one of Lorenzo Monaco's greatest achievements and a fundamental milestone in the history of Italian Gothic painting. Simone Martini painted an identical subject in 1333 (currently in

98

the Uffizi), yet Lorenzo Monaco's Annunciation is distinguished by a tighter rhythm and more elaborate presentation where the decorative choices (note the laces around the angel's ankles) aim at creating spiritual tension.

99 - **Maestro della Madonna Straus** (Florence, data from the late XIV to early XV centuries)
Annunciation. Inv. 1890 n° 3146.
This painting is usually attributed to an anonymous painter who was close to Agnolo Gaddi and dubbed "Maestro della Madonna Straus from a painting of a Madonna and Child which was formerly part of the Straus" collection and today belongs to the Houston (Texas) Museum. The date ranges between 1390/95 and the early years of the XV century. It was brought to the Accademia from the hospital of Sta Maria Nuova, after having been moved from the leper hospital of S. Eusebio sul Prato near Florence.

99

100

100 - **Maestro della Madonna Straus** (Florence, data from the late XIV to early XV centuries)
Pietà With Symbols of the Passion. Inv. Storage n° 14.
This painting, by the same anonymous artist who did the Annunciation in the other room, comes from the destroyed church of St. Pier Martire (Florence). Because of stylistic similarities with the Pietà dated 1405 which is in the Warsaw museum, this painting is also considered to have been painted around that time.
The subject, which is quite rare in other periods, was quite common around 1400 when a large part of the population was overwhelmed by a fear of turn-of-the-century-catastrophes and therefore, penitence and meditation about death became widespread practices.

101 - **Giovanni Toscani** (Florence 1370-1430)
The Incredulity of St. Thomas. Inv. 1890 n° 457.
The painting was brought to the Accademia in 1815, probably from the Tribunale della Mercatanzia that was built between 1419 and 1420. The trends of the period are evident in the painting's style as well as in the accentuated Gothicism of the drapings (see the rich and abundant cloth on Christ's arm) and the isolated monumentality of the figures. The artist was Giovanni Toscani, a Florentine painter, long known as the "Maestro della Crocefissione Griggs" and only officially identified in 1966.

101

102

102 - **Giovanni Toscani** (Florence, c. 1370-1430)
Crucfixion, The Stigmata of St. Francis, and The Miracle of St. Nicholas of Bari. Inv. 1890 n° 6089 and 3333. The cuspid and compartment of the predella were part of the polyptych in the Ardinghelli Chapel in the church of the Sta Trinita in Florence. The chapel, dedicated to St. Nicholas was frescoed by Giovanni Toscani beween 1423 and 1424. Therefore, these paintings must also date from the same period, as do those in other museums, which have been acknowledged as having been part of the same polyptych.
For many years Giovanni Toscani was known as the "Maestro della Crocefissione Griggs", from the title of his major painting, until 1966 when valuable documents came to light and made it possible to identify him.

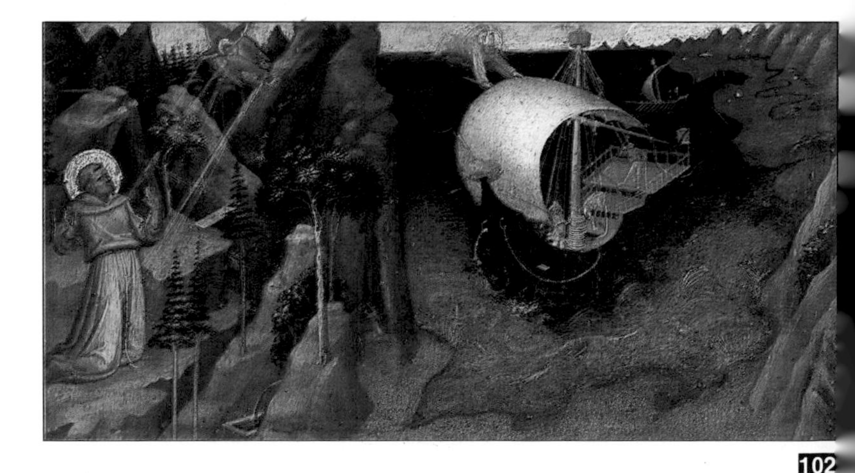

102

103 - **Maestro di Borgo alla Collina** (data from the first decades of the XV century)

Madonna and Child with Saints. Inv. 1890 n° 478.

The painting can be dated around 1420, within the context of the work of a painter (perhaps the so-called "Maestro di Borgo alla Collina") who combined a mature Gothic style, as seen in the fluid and redundant drapings, accented volumes, especially in the

103

Child's muscular little limbs that could not be justified prior to the twenties and the advent of Masaccio.

The Icon Collection

The Accademia Gallery also has a fine collection of Russian and Byzantine icons, most of which were acquired by the Grand Dukes of Lorraine. The collection, which had been in warehouses or other inaccessible places for nearly two hundred years, is now united and open to the public on the first floor.
Although the quality is not consistent, these works are important evidence of the eighteenth century passion for collecting and specifically of the dynasty that succeeded the Medici rule in Florence.

104

104 - **Andrea Rico da Candia** (data in Italy from the first half of the XV cent.)
Madonna and Child. Inv. 1890 n° 3886.
The iconography of this painting from the church of the monastery of S. Girolamo in Fiesole is quite unusual. On either side of the Madonna and Child there are angels holding symbols of the Passion. Andrea Rico certainly spread this mode of depicting the Virgin (if he did not invent it himself) which may be from Crete. The aim was to recall the final purpose of Christ's Incarnation, even within the context of a traditionally sweet and reassuring scene such as that of the Madonna holding her Son.

105 - **Basili Grasnov** (Stroganov School, XVIII cent.)
Saint Catherine. Inv. 1890 n° 5979.
The old Russian inscription reads "The martyrdom of Catherine of Christ". The icon is a copy of an earlier one dating from the XVIII

105

106

century with some modem stylistic touches that should not be overlooked.

106 - **Russian School** (XVII century)
The Beheading of the Baptist. Inv. 1890 n° 9355.
The gilded, and hammered silver frame bears an old Russian inscription "Beheading of the Baptist". On the right we can see St. John being led to his death, and on the right the decapitated Saint. The style is a copy of the Novgorod school, done in the late XVII century, perhaps by an artist from the Stroganov School.

107 - **Russian School** (XVII century)
Dormitio Virginis. Inv. 1890 n° 6147.
Like the other icons in the room, this one is from the collection of

107

the grand dukes of Lorraine which was transferred to the Uffizi in 1771. Some were displayed when the Uffizi Gallery was reorganized between 1780 and 1782; others were returned to the grand dukes in 1783. However, even those on display were soon (1796) removed and stored at the Villa at Castello. Only in 1985 when the first floor of the Accademia gallery was being set up was the entire group brought together, restored and put on view. It is quite diversified as to origins, artists and quality, but the collection is the fruit of the curiosity of an enthusiast rather than an expert. Its importance, however, is in the fact that it represents a very particular episode in the history of European art collections.

index of the artists

the rooms